The Complete Guide to Investing in Undervalued Properties

The Complete Guide to Investing in Undervalued Properties

STEVE BERGES

McGraw-Hill

New York   Chicago   San Francisco   Lisbon   London
Madrid   Mexico City   Milan   New Delhi   San Juan
Seoul   Singapore   Sydney   Toronto

1 2 3 4 5 6 7 8 9 0   FGR/FGR   0 9 8 7 6 5 4

ISBN 0-07-144580-3

This publication is designed to provide accurate and authoritative information in regard to the subject matter covered. It is sold with the understanding that neither the author nor the publisher is engaged in rendering legal, accounting, futures/securities trading, or other professional service. If legal advice or other expert assistance is required, the services of a competent professional person should be sought.

—From a Declaration of Principles jointly adopted by a Committee
of the American Bar Association and a Committee of Publishers

McGraw-Hill books are available at special quantity discounts to use as premiums and sales promotions, or for use in corporate training programs. For more information, please write to the Director of Special Sales, Professional Publishing, McGraw-Hill, Two Penn Plaza, New York, NY 10121-2298. Or contact your local bookstore.

This book is printed on recycled, acid-free paper containing a minimum of 50% recycled, de-inked fiber.

Library of Congress Cataloging-in-Publication Data

Berges, Steve.
    The complete guide to investing in undervalued properties / by Steve Berges.
—1st ed.
        p. cm.
    Includes bibliographical references and index.
    ISBN 0-07-144580-3 (alk. paper)
  1. Real estate investment. I. Title.
    HD1382.5.B464 2005
    332.63'24—dc22   2004025798

Contents

Contents

Contents

Part 3 How to Use Options to Purchase Undervalued Properties

Contents

The Complete Guide to Investing in Undervalued Properties

PART 1

Fundamental Principles of Real Estate Valuation

1

Investing in Undervalued Properties

Introduction

All successful businesses that deal in the reselling of some type of tangible goods share one thing in common. They buy low and sell high. In the automotive industry, for example, thousands of parts are purchased from suppliers all over the world and assembled together into various working components that will each perform a function according to its respective design specifications. The components are then assembled with the utmost precision and in perfect order. The resulting product is a finely tuned automobile that will carry consumers safely to their destinations in comfort and style. The automotive manufacturer purchases the parts required to assemble the car at wholesale prices. As each component moves down the assembly line and is assembled with other components, the car begins to take shape. Wheels are added to a chassis, then an engine and a drive train. Later come the body, interior seats, and control panels, until at last the car is finished. At the end of the assembly line, the new car finally rolls off and is then made ready to ship to a dealer. The dealer will in turn sell the car to the end user, the consumer.

At each stage of progression, value is added to the automobiles. The suppliers who make the individual parts from raw materials, such as plastic, aluminum, and steel, add value and in turn sell for a profit to the automobile manufacturer. The manufacturer then adds value by assembling the many individual parts into components and finally into working automobiles. The automobiles are then sold for a profit to a dealer, who purchases the cars at what is considered to be wholesale prices. The dealer carries many different styles, designs, and colors of automobiles in inventory that are supplied by the manufacturer. The dealer then resells the automobiles for a profit to consumers, who are the end users of the product. At each stage of progression, the newly added value is reflected in the price of the parts or vehicle. This allows all of the participants to profit from their respective capital invested in manufacturing facilities, equipment, and showroom floors. Without a profit incentive, operations would cease and the investors' capital would be employed in other industries or businesses.

Real estate investors who enjoy a high degree of success are similar to their counterparts in the automotive industry and share a common element. They buy real estate, such as single-family houses, at wholesale prices and, at some point in the future, resell the property at retail prices. In other words, real estate investors are merchants who deal in various types of property, buying low and selling high. That's all there is to it. Sounds easy enough doesn't it? To make money in real estate, all one has to do is to buy low and sell high. Is it really as simple as that? The fundamental issue for each and every transaction centers around the question, "What is considered to be a low price, a moderate price, and a high price for a particular piece of real estate?" The precept *value is relative* makes answering this question difficult.

Investing in Undervalued Properties

In a previous book I wrote entitled *The Complete Guide to Investing in Rental Properties* (New York: McGraw-Hill, 2004), I explained the idea of relative value by citing the example of shopping for a new car. When shopping for a new car, you're likely to start by comparing prices, makes, and models advertised in the newspaper. After narrowing your search down to the two or three cars that appear to best fit your needs, you're then likely to begin shopping at several dealers to determine who is offering the best price. All other things being equal, the car with the lowest price is also the one with the best value.

Comparison shopping for a house is no different than comparison shopping for a car. After perusing the advertising pages of the local newspaper, you begin the task of looking at houses in the price range and area that fit your needs the best. Similar to shopping for a car, once you've narrowed your search down to two or three houses, price becomes even more important, and all other things being equal, the house with the lowest price is also the one with the best value.

Using the logic described in this example, we have established the precept that, indeed, value is relative. The notion that value is relative is essential for investors not only to understand, but to practice and apply when making decisions as they relate to the analysis of real estate investments. Without this knowledge, it would be very easy to overpay for a property. Investors should take care to factor this precept in when analyzing potential purchase opportunities. With the demand for real estate increasing at a record pace, property prices have only one way to go—up. As prices continue to increase, value often suffers. As investors migrate from the stock market to the real estate market at an ever-increasing rate, the need to understand value is greater than ever. Just as buying high-flying stocks with no regard to intrinsic values resulted in thousands of investors losing their life savings, so will buying real estate with reckless disregard to property values result in a similar outcome. In order to understand whether or not a property is over, under, or properly valued, investors must first have a basic understanding of the principles of valuation as they apply to real estate. In other words, investors must be able to determine what constitutes the true value for a particular piece of real estate, whether it is a tract of vacant land, a single-family house, or a multifamily apartment building. Then, and only then, can sound financial decisions be made.

This book is organized into four primary parts that will provide investors with a thorough and comprehensive understanding of how to locate and purchase undervalued real estate properties. Part 1, Fundamental Principles of Real Estate Valuation, focuses on the principles of real estate valuation and will enable readers to more fully understand what constitutes a poor, average, or good value. Part 2, How to Find Undervalued Properties, provides readers with a complete guide to finding undervalued properties and includes numerous methods, stratagems, and techniques for finding real estate at bargain prices. Part 3, How to Use Options to Purchase Undervalued Properties, centers around key, low risk techniques for buying real estate with options and other low down payment strategies. Finally, in Part 4, Epilogue, you'll learn about several effective precepts that can help you achieve your absolute best in life. When properly applied, these laws can help propel you to accomplish extraordinary success in real estate or any other endeavor you choose to pursue. The methods presented throughout this book embody several principles that will unlock the doors leading to success if you will just turn the key. Study these principles carefully, then put on the armor of success, and you will discover a power within yourself that will enable you to attain all that you desire in life.

Five Ways to Benefit from Owning Real Estate

Individuals today have more choices than ever in which to invest their savings. Some of these include debt instruments, such as bonds and certificates of deposit. Other choices include stocks, real estate, futures, options, and even precious metals such as gold and silver. Among the many choices available, real estate is unquestionably one of the best asset classes an investor can own. There are numerous ways to benefit from owning real estate, including price appreciation, principal reduction, and tax benefits. Other benefits of owning real estate include the ability to generate income as well as to maximize leverage opportunities. (See Figure 1.1.)

Five Ways to Benefit from Owning Real Estate

1. Price appreciation
2. Reduction in principal
3. Tax savings
4. Income
5. Leverage

Figure 1.1

The first way investors can benefit from owning real estate is through price appreciation. Changes in price or value occur for two primary reasons: an increase in the supply of money and increases in demand that are not correspondingly met by increases in supply. The Federal Reserve Board, or Fed, is responsible for changes in the nation's money supply. Increases in the money supply result in the devaluation of the dollar and the increase, or inflation, of prices. As more dollars flood the market and become available to purchase goods, the value of the dollar decreases further. I can remember, for example, when it only cost 25 cents to go to the movies. The going rate now ranges anywhere from $6 to $10 a ticket depending on where you live. When I was a young boy, not only did it cost less to get into the movies, but the cost of food, gasoline, and housing, as well as all other goods, was much less. The subsequent rise in prices is a result of the ever-increasing supply of money, otherwise known as *inflation*. The second component of price appreciation reflects changes in the demand for housing. Positive changes in economic conditions, such as a low unemployment rate and low interest rates, have contributed significantly to the demand for housing. Other notable factors that have contributed to the demand for housing are the growth in the nation's population because of the birth of children and a steady flow of immigrants into the country. Census data indicates that the nation's population is growing at the rate of approximately 3.5 to 4 million residents a year. Additionally, constraints in supply because of limited land availability and increasing governmental regulations have also placed upward pressure on prices, thereby contributing to the price appreciation that occurs in real estate.

The second way to benefit from the ownership of real estate occurs through the reduction in the principal loan balance. This benefit applies primarily to investors who have tenants paying for their income-producing property, such as rental houses or apartment buildings. Each month, as the loan payment is made, a portion of the payment is applied toward the interest and the principal. Since reducing the principal means reducing the loan balance, as the payments are made month after month and year after year, the balance will eventually be paid in full. In the early years of repayment, most of the payment is applied toward the interest. Over time, however, more and more of the payment is applied toward the principal of the loan as the respective proportions gradually begin to reverse. The rate of interest charged has a dynamic impact on not only the amount of payment assessed each month, but also the point at which the crossover occurs between the amount of interest charged and the amount of principal applied to reduce the loan balance. In other words, the point of crossover is the point at which the principal portion of the loan payment begins to exceed the interest portion of the loan payment. To illustrate this point, let's look at two different examples using the same loan terms with the exception of the interest rate. The following list shows the loan information that is used in Figure 1.2. Note that the point of crossover occurs just after Year 16.

Loan Amount = $100,000
Loan Period = 30 years
Interest Rate = 5%
Annual Payment = $6,442
Point of Crossover = Year 16

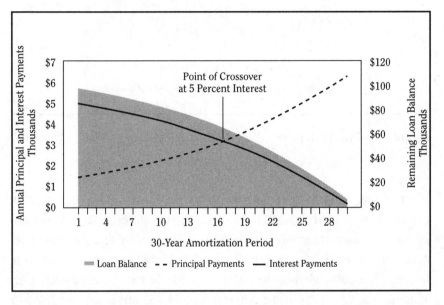

Figure 1.2 Principal, Interest, and Loan Balance Dynamics at 5 Percent Interest

Now take a moment to study the loan terms of Figure 1.3.

Loan Amount = $100,000
Loan Period = 30 years
Interest Rate = 10%
Annual Payment = $10,531
Point of Crossover = Year 23

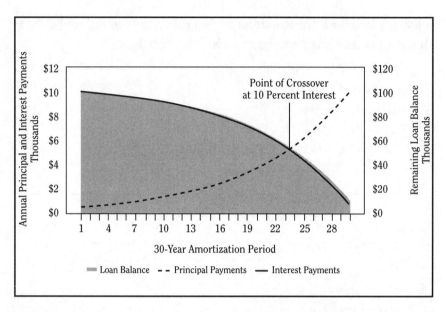

Figure 1.3   Principal, Interest, and Loan Balance Dynamics at 10 Percent Interest

The point of crossover in this example doesn't occur until some time after Year 23 because of the higher rate of interest charged over the life of the loan. Moreover, note the difference in annual payments between Figures 1.2 and 1.3. In Figure 1.2, $6,442 is required each year to repay the note; whereas in Figure 1.3, $10,531 is required each year. This represents a significant difference of $4,089 annually, or $122,670 over the 30-year loan period!

Whether a loan with a 5 percent or a 10 percent interest rate is obtained, the reduction in the principal loan balance is an important benefit of owning income-producing real estate. In the examples illustrated in Figures 1.2 and 1.3, the loans will be completely paid down in exactly 360 months if equal payments are made over their duration. At the end of the 30-year period, the investor would own the property free and clear. The best thing about this benefit is that it is the tenants who are making the payments each month, month after month, thereby reducing the loan balance until it is finally paid in full. The tenants, for all practical purposes, become partners in your success!

The third way to benefit from the ownership of real estate is brought about by a reduction in federal and state taxes. The Internal Revenue Service, or IRS, mandates that income-producing property be depreciated over a specific time period. Depreciation can be a little confusing to investors who are new to the concept. The important thing to understand, however, is that it is a calculation made primarily for tax purposes and has no impact on the actual cash flow from property. A reduction in tax liability is a very real benefit and, depending on how many properties are owned, depreciation and other write-offs can easily reduce an investor's tax liability to zero!

Another way to benefit from the ownership of real estate is derived from the net positive cash flow realized from the monthly payments made by income-producing tenants. The net cash flow is the portion remaining after subtracting all expenses from gross revenues. Investors of income-producing real estate should strive to purchase only those properties that meet two criteria. The first criterion is that a rental property is priced at or below fair market value, and the second criterion is that the property produces a proper cash flow. For an income-producing property to have a proper cash flow, it should have sufficient revenue to produce a residual on an ongoing basis. This means that after all expenses for a given period have been paid, including PITI (principal, interest, taxes, and insurance), an investor should have something left over. A net positive cash flow from income-producing property is yet another way investors can benefit by owning real estate. Refer to Figures 1.2 and 1.3, where 5 and 10 percent were used respectively. Recall that the difference in annual debt service was $4,089. On a loan of only $100,000, this represents a material difference that would, in all probability, create a negative cash flow at the higher interest rate. This would depend on the rental income the market supports in the area where the house is located. But an investor purchasing a similar property with 5 percent financing in place would have a clear advantage over the investor in the same market with 10 percent financing.

Finally, investors can also benefit from the ownership of real estate through the remarkable leverage that can be achieved when acquiring property. The principle of leverage enables buyers to purchase a sizable asset with very little money of their own through a combination of debt and equity. Buyers can essentially borrow most of the funds needed to purchase real estate, which, in turn, allows them to capitalize on the returns earned by the entire asset. The return on an investor's capital is then magnified since the proportion of personal funds invested to funds borrowed is typically much less.

In order for leverage to be applied, a fulcrum must be used. A *fulcrum* is defined as the support on which a lever turns. As it applies to real estate, a fulcrum represents the use of other people's money. On one end of the lever is an investor's initial capital outlay, however small it may be, and on the other end of the lever is the real estate being levered up. It is the fulcrum that enables purchasers to apply the law of leverage. The OPM principle, or other people's money principle, allows investors to maximize the use of leverage. The primary objective for investors is to control as much real estate as possible while using as little of their own money as possible. The more access an investor has to other people's money, the greater the degree of leverage that can be achieved, and the greater the degree of leverage that can be achieved, the higher the potential return on an investment.

For those of you who may be first-time investors, leverage can be especially important because, oftentimes, individuals just getting started have the least amount of cash to work with. Constraints on the availability of your personal cash need not prevent you from becoming a successful real estate investor. Rather, the lack of capital when just getting started can actually benefit you by forcing you to seek alternative means of financing. Once you get in the habit of looking for creative ways to finance the purchase of a property, you'll discover that even after you have the means to structure a conventional transaction with 10 percent or so down, you'll still look for creative ways to put a deal together with less or no money down.

Economic Impact of Housing

To say that the financial impact of the housing industry on the nation's economy is significant would be an understatement. In fact, in a report issued by the National Association of Home Builders (NAHB) entitled "Housing Facts, Figures, and Trends 2004," the combined economic effects of single-family construction, multifamily construction, and remodeling account for 15 percent of the gross domestic product, or GDP, and as much as one-third of GDP in periods of an economic downturn, as was demonstrated in recent years. According to the report, the construction of 1,000 single-family homes generates on average:

2,448 jobs in construction and construction-related industries

Approximately $79.4 million in wages

More than $42.5 million in federal, state, and local tax revenues and fees

Moreover, the construction of 1,000 multifamily homes generates on average:

1,030 jobs in construction and construction-related industries

Approximately $33.5 million in wages

More than $17.8 million in federal, state, and local tax revenues and fees

The report issued by the NAHB asserts that the spending doesn't necessarily stop after a new home is purchased. In fact, the report indicates a spillover effect that occurs over a broader range of industries than just housing. For instance, families moving into new homes often purchase new furnishings to go into them. This could include a new bedroom set, furniture for the family room, a big-screen TV, appliances for the kitchen, dining room table and chairs, and most anything in between. The spending doesn't stop there either because the kids will surely need a new playground set for the backyard. Dad will most likely want a new lawnmower, Mom will want new dinnerware for the kitchen and china for the dining room, and Fido will have to have a new place to sleep, along with a new dinner bowl. And so it is that the spending spree goes on and on. This spending spree does not occur only among purchasers of new homes, but also among buyers of existing housing and renters who have recently moved. In short, any time a household moves from one location to another, a spillover effect is created among other industries. The NAHB quantifies the industry-related spending that occurs in the following excerpt from its report.

> *Spending on a Newly Purchased Home.* Housing's economic impact doesn't end when the home is sold and the new owners move in. In fact, housing continues to be an economic force long after the sale is closed. In the first 12 months after purchasing a newly built home, owners spend an average of $8,905 to furnish, decorate and improve their homes. Buyers of existing homes spend $3,766 more than nonmoving homeowners during the 12 months after purchasing the home, and renters spend significant amounts on furnishing their new homes. New home buyers are more likely to spend their money on improvements such as landscaping, decks, patios, fences and driveways. Buyers of existing homes are more likely to spend money on remodeling rooms, plumbing repairs, and heating or air conditioning. Although it is highly decentralized and made up primarily of small businesses, the collective might of the housing industry is huge, accounting for about 15 cents of every dollar spent in America during a typical year. [NAHB, "Housing Facts, Figures, and Trends, 2004"]

The impact of the housing market has been, and will continue to be, a driving force in the nation's economy. According to the "Flow of Funds" report issued by the Federal Reserve in late 2003, housing accounts for 31 percent of total household wealth in the United States. This represents the largest share of an average homeowner's wealth, topping other categories such as pension funds, mutual funds, and savings deposits as illus-

trated in Figure 1.4. The total value of the nation's housing stock is estimated to be in excess of $15 trillion. Homeowners' share of that accounts
for over half, with approximately $8 trillion in home equity.

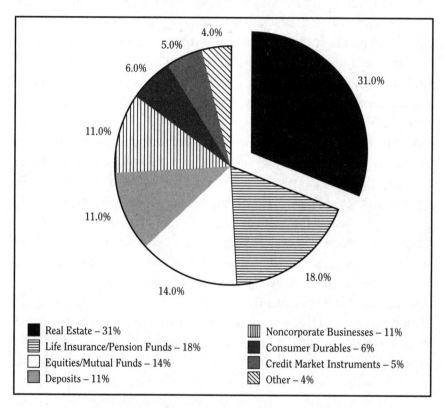

Figure 1.4   Total Household Wealth, 2003

Real Estate Market Outlook

The robust outlook for the real estate market over the coming decade
continues to remain quite positive for several key reasons. First, according to Dr. David Berson, vice president and chief economist for Fannie
Mae, the forecast for the average real GDP growth is 3.4 to 3.5 percent.
This compares to 3.2 percent during the 1990s. Another reason is the

forecast for fixed-rate mortgages. According to Dr. Berson, interest rates should taper off at about 7.2 to 7.5 percent. This compares to a less favorable rate of 7.9 percent throughout the 1990s. A more favorable interest rate environment for housing is almost always a bullish indicator for housing. Also, as previously mentioned, census data indicates the nation's population is growing at the rate of approximately 3.5 to 4 million residents a year. Finally, constraints in supply due to limited land availability and increasing governmental regulations have placed upward pressure on prices, thereby contributing to the price appreciation that occurs in real estate.

While the economic outlook for the next decade at the national level appears to be quite promising, participants in the real estate market also can capitalize on regional trends. For example, by purchasing houses in those areas that are experiencing high rates of growth, investors are able to enjoy the benefits of higher rates of price appreciation as well as quicker turnaround times. For an investor who is buying and selling as opposed to buying and holding, the resell time is critical. Resell time is typically measured by the average number of days on the market it takes to sell a house and is frequently tracked by services such as the Multiple Listing Service, or MLS. For those investors who are just getting started investing in real estate, it may be difficult to invest in markets other than those within a close proximity to where you live. As your capital base grows, however, you can graduate into larger properties and begin to utilize services such as property management firms to help you manage projects in high growth areas such as Atlanta, Georgia. Atlanta has consistently been at the very top of the rankings in terms of growth for several years. Take a moment to review Table 1.1, which shows the number of permits issued in the top 25 markets for the construction of new homes.

Investors also can study the broader trend by looking at the population growth in states. In general, the data indicates that most of the growth is occurring in those states that enjoy a warmer climate. This is for two primary reasons. First, speaking from experience, people don't like being cold. I've lived in climates at both extremes. In the southern

Investing in Undervalued Properties

Table 1.1   Top 25 Metropolitan Markets for Single-Family Permits in 2003

		Permits Issued	
		First 9 Months	12 Months
Rank	City	Actual	Estimated
1	Atlanta, GA	40,580	54,107
2	Phoenix-Mesa, AZ	35,480	47,307
3	Riverside-San Bernadino, CA	28,140	37,520
4	Houston, TX	26,820	35,760
5	Washington, DC	24,580	32,773
6	Las Vegas, NV	23,190	30,920
7	Chicago, IL	23,090	30,787
8	Dallas, TX	20,990	27,987
9	Orlando, FL	16,670	22,227
10	Tampa-St. Petersburg, FL	15,440	20,587
11	Minneapolis-St. Paul, MN	15,060	20,080
12	Charlotte-Gastonia-Rock Hill, NC	13,430	17,907
13	Sacramento, CA	12,850	17,133
14	Detroit, MI	11,470	15,293
15	Ft. Worth-Arlington, TX	10,870	14,493
16	Raleigh-Durham-Chapel Hill, NC	10,640	14,187
17	Indianapolis, IN	10,150	13,533
18	Jacksonville, Fl	9,830	13,107
19	Denver, CO	9,690	12,920
20	St. Louis, MO	9,170	12,227
21	Philadelphia, PA	9,130	12,173
22	Columbus, OH	9,120	12,160
23	Kansas City, KS	8,950	11,933
24	Nashville, TN	8,780	11,707
25	Seattle-Bellevue-Everett, WA	8,620	11,493
	Total	412,740	550,320

region of Texas, although it was hot and humid, I never had to worry
about shoveling the snow off my driveway or getting stuck in an ice
storm. In Michigan, on the other hand, I do. In fact, winter conditions
can be so severe that motorists have to take extra precautions in the
event they become stranded while traveling. If their cars break down or
run off the road due to icy conditions, for example, subzero tempera-
tures can quickly take their toll. The result can be fatal. The second primary reason southern states have the largest increase in population is
because of their proximity to Mexico, where immigration into the bordering states is high. Demographic trends in the southern states shows
a large influx of Hispanics over the last 20 to 30 years. This trend is driv-
en primarily by the comparatively favorable economic conditions in the
United States. Take a moment to review Table 1.2, which lists the 10
states with the largest increases in population.

Table 1.2   Top 10 States with Largest Increase in Population, 1990 to 2000

Rank	State	Population (in millions)		Change in Population	
Rank	State	1990	2000	Number	Percent
1	California	29.76	33.87	4.11	13.81%
2	Texas	16.99	20.85	3.86	22.72%
3	Florida	12.94	15.98	3.04	23.49%
4	Georgia	6.48	8.19	1.71	26.39%
5	Arizona	3.66	5.13	1.47	40.16%
6	North Carolina	6.63	8.05	1.42	21.42%
7	Washington	4.87	5.89	1.02	20.94%
8	Colorado	3.29	4.30	1.01	30.70%
9	New York	17.99	18.98	0.99	5.50%
10	Virginia	6.19	7.08	0.89	14.38%
	Total	108.80	128.32	19.52	17.94%

While Table 1.2 shows the largest increases in population by the actual number of people moving into a state, Table 1.3 illustrates the largest increase in population by the percentage change. The two trends are still very similar with the greatest increases occurring primarily in southern regions. Notice, however, the cluster of states in the West extending from Arizona and Nevada northward to Idaho. These regions tend to attract individuals and businesses alike by offering lower tax structures than many other states. As businesses relocate to take advantage of tax incentives, many of their employees will naturally go with them. The result is that by offering lower tax rates, these states are able to attract more businesses and individuals and actually end up increasing the tax base rather than lowering it. You might call it the Wal-Mart effect. If people can save money by shopping at Wal-Mart rather than at the local five and dime, then that's where they will shop. Wal-Mart more

Table 1.3   Top 10 States with Largest Percentage Increase in Population, 1990 to 2000

		Population (in millions)		Change in Population	
Rank	State	1990	2000	Number	Percent
1	Nevada	1.20	2.00	0.80	66.67%
2	Arizona	3.66	5.13	1.47	40.16%
3	Colorado	3.29	4.30	1.01	30.70%
4	Utah	1.72	2.23	0.51	29.65%
5	Idaho	1.01	1.29	0.28	27.72%
6	Georgia	6.48	8.19	1.71	26.39%
7	Florida	12.94	15.98	3.04	23.49%
8	Texas	16.99	20.85	3.86	22.72%
9	North Carolina	6.63	8.05	1.42	21.42%
10	Washington	4.87	5.89	1.02	20.94%
	Total	58.79	73.91	15.12	25.94%

than makes up for in volume what it gives up in percentage terms. Its business model is to operate on thinner profit margins, but at a much higher volume. This strategy has enabled it to trounce the competition while simultaneously becoming one of the most successful discount stores in the world. Now take a moment to review Table 1.3, which shows the top 10 states with the largest percentage increases in population.

Applying the principles of value is not exclusive to the real estate industry. They are, in fact, fundamental to the success of any business. To maximize shareholder value, investors must take every precaution to employ capital in the most efficient manner possible. In order for capital to be efficiently employed, every effort must be made to seek value. If business owners continuously overpay for goods and services, shareholder value will inevitably be compromised. The business owners who ignore this cardinal rule will ultimately be replaced by those who respect it.

Aspirations of Wealth

I'd like to share with you a recent experience I had which demonstrates that many people feel conflicted about aspiring to wealth. In this example, the conflicted feelings arise from religious and spiritual beliefs, but this conflict can be secular as well. A question was posed to our Sunday school class by the teacher, "Should we aspire to wealth and is this a righteous endeavor?" After raising my hand, the Sunday school teacher called on me to share my thoughts on the matter. I replied that, in my opinion, aspiring to wealth was and is acceptable and that yes, it is a righteous endeavor. I shared a couple of examples of the good that wealth created by us can do. It can build churches and temples to bless and sanctify the lives of others, it can build hospitals and medical facilities to heal the sick, it can build schools and universities to teach the uneducated, and it can build machinery and equipment to harvest and provide food for the world's population. Without wealth, these things are not possible. A few minutes later, a young man about the age of 22 or so raised his hand to share his belief and, much to my surprise, took the opposite viewpoint. In his opinion, we should not seek riches but instead should only seek God's kingdom and nothing more. About that time, class was over so I didn't have the opportunity to respond to this young man's comments by clarifying my position. It is for this reason that I feel the necessity to write this section at this time, not only for his benefit, but for the benefit of my readers as well.

Authors Mark Hansen and Robert Allen address this very issue in the *New York Times* bestseller *The One Minute Millionaire: The Enlightened Way to Wealth* (Harmony, 2002). In the introductory chapter, the authors outline what they refer to as the "principles of the enlightened millionaire" (pp. xvi–xvii). The underlying philosophy of the enlightened millionaire is that while wealth increases the degree of physical, spiritual, and monetary freedom an individual enjoys, along with that freedom comes responsibility. Authors Hansen and Allen further elaborate by discussing the following principles. The first principle emphasizes to "do no harm" by not engaging in wealth-building activities that are destructive in nature. The second principle is just the opposite, to "do much good," and emphasizes the need to create wealth while simultaneously improving the lives of others. The third principle asserts that those individuals who pursue wealth should "operate out of stewardship." The authors write:

> Enlightened Millionaires are stewards over their financial blessings—enjoying the privileges of financial success while creating an ongoing legacy to bless others. Many Enlightened Millionaires feel a personal "calling" to provide support to one or more specific causes (such as Jerry Lewis and muscular dystrophy). The goal is not to amass personal wealth for its own sake, but to ultimately create a perpetual giving fund to support worthy causes. In other words, your wealth is not just for you (selfish), but for blessing the lives of many people (selfless). The first proof of your commitment to make money to bless other people is to give at least the first 10% away.

We want to inspire a million millionaires to give 10% of all they earn each year back to their communities—to improve the lives of others around them. When this happens, it will generate BILLIONS of dollars focused on improving the well-being of humankind.

Whether you start out by donating or otherwise contributing 1 percent of your increase or 10 percent, the idea is to give something back so that those around you might benefit. While efforts to uplift others should be performed with no thought of receiving anything in return, the truth is that because you have gone out of your way to help those who are in need, the law of reciprocity prescribed by nature suggests that the good you have done for others will come back to you a hundredfold.

In essence, within each of us lies the power to accomplish great and noble tasks. We have all been given the gift of agency, and with that gift, we are free to choose who we will become. Although we are all destined to greatness, we must exercise our free agency in a manner that will help us fulfill our destiny. One way we can do that is by giving of our means to bless and enrich the lives of others, to lift up those around us who stand in need. Each selfless act of kindness magnifies the charity within our own hearts and increases our capacity to love others and to accept them for who they are. These acts of kindness need not be some grand event on the scale of magnitude, but rather, they are the small and simple things we do each day. As I write these very words, my two-year-old son, Benjamin, has wandered in. It's late at night and he is looking for the comfort of his daddy's arms to rock him to sleep. My little Ben and I share a special bond of love, a bond that pierces the thin veil of eternity. I gladly and affectionately cradle him in the security of my arms while taking a break from writing. These are the small and simple acts of kindness that shape who we are, and who we are to become. It would have been just as easy for me to send my little Ben to his mother and not to have taken time for him. These are the moments in life, however, that I truly cherish. These are the moments that, once they are gone, will be gone forever. I will never get them back. These are the moments that are irreplaceable and priceless. These are the seemingly insignificant moments that will strengthen the bonds of love my son and I share. These are the habits and patterns that will keep him coming back to me over the course of his life, not only for comfort, but for advice, for counsel, for encouragement, and, above all, for love.

To my young friend at church, I say to you that the notions of aspiring to wealth and aspiring to seek the kingdom of God are *not* mutually exclusive. One *can* do both at the same time. To seek *only* wealth would be an injustice and a gross misuse of our talents. We can instead seek to find the proper balance in our lives in all that we do. To suggest that we cannot aspire to wealth and seek a higher and nobler purpose at the same time is like saying that we cannot play basketball or baseball and seek a higher purpose at the same time, or like saying that we cannot seek a higher education and seek a higher purpose in life at the same time. To my young friend and to all of you, I say *balance is the key*. Have you ever driven a car in which the wheels were out of balance? For those of you who may have experienced driving a car in this condition, you know that the steering wheel can vibrate as you're driving, especially under certain conditions, such as when a certain speed is reached. The vibration in the steering wheel is caused by the slight vibrations from the out-of-balance wheels that are then transmitted through the steering system and eventually reach the driver's hands. If the wheels are severely out of balance, the vibration is likely to be enough to be quite noticeable, causing the entire car to shake. Like the car, when our lives are out of balance, things seem to not go as smoothly and give us a rough ride as we go about our business throughout each day. In order to enjoy a smooth and comfortable ride, we must carefully balance all that we do. Maintaining a life that is in its proper balance will then enable us to reach the potential that lies within.

Several years ago, I planted 10 Colorado blue spruce trees along the perimeter of my yard to serve as a natural boundary as well as for screening and beautification purposes between my house and the neighbors' houses on each side of mine. Although each tree measured exactly 4 feet in height at the time they were planted, today they range in size and health from about 5 feet and almost dead to as tall as 15 feet and very healthy. I have come to learn over the years through careful observation of their growth that there is a slight difference each tree receives in the amount of water, nutrients, and sunlight. The smallest of these trees is planted in a low-lying area of the lawn where water collects and consequently causes the tree to receive an overabundance of water, as its root system remains saturated. Furthermore, the tree was planted in clay-like soil, which not only lacks the proper nutrients, but also prevents its roots from growing freely. Finally, this tree is planted on the southeast side of my house where it is exposed to the bright summer sun. The elements that promote the health of any plant or tree—water, nutrients, and sun—are clearly out of balance for this ailing tree. In stark contrast to this is the largest of the 10 trees, measuring close to 15 feet in height. It sits up slightly higher where the water has room to run off, it was planted in superior soil, and it is situated on the northwest side of my house where it receives just the right amount of sunlight. The three elements that promote health for plant life are clearly in balance for this vibrant and beautiful spruce tree, as it receives just the right amount of water, nutrients, and sunlight. The life sustaining elements in this example that are in their proper balance have allowed the healthy tree to grow three times as large as the sickly tree in which these elements are out of balance. And so it is with each of us. Our lives are centered around a myriad of responsibilities, including family, church, work, school, social, civic, and many other duties that can sometimes seem to overwhelm us. It has been my experience that by striving to keep my own life in its proper balance among my many responsibilities, I have enjoyed a greater sense of peace and control. I no longer torment myself with guilt because I said no to one activity so that I could say yes to another activity. It's okay to say no sometimes, especially when it means saying yes to another worthwhile endeavor. As you read and study the real estate topics presented in this book, I encourage you to keep the principle of balance in mind, for you, too, are destined for greatness.

2

Understanding Real Estate Value

Fundamentals of Valuation Analysis

If wealth is a measurement of success, icon Warren Buffett is the epitome of that success. Buffett, one of the richest men in the world, has earned the reputation for being the greatest value investor of all time. Buffett is well known for his remarkable ability to recognize undervalued asset classes and has built his fortune centered around those principles. Buffett is not beholden to any one asset class, but instead employs capital among a variety of classes. He has successfully invested in insurance, stocks, bonds, real estate, and precious metals, to name but a few. Buffett possesses the courage and insight that few others do. He has, for example, invested time and time again in various asset classes when very few, if any, other investors would even go near them. Buffett goes where the crowd does not. Chances are, if everyone else is jumping on the bandwagon to get into an investment (such as stocks), Buffett has already sold and is on his way to the next opportunity. Today Warren Buffett has earned the respect of his peers, and rightfully so. There are even those who are known as "Buffett watchers" who essentially follow his every move. If Warren Buffett is buying silver, the Buffett watchers buy silver. If Warren Buffett is selling stocks, the Buffett watchers sell stocks. Warren Buffett has been so successful applying the principles of value that the two have practically become synonymous with each other. Mention Warren Buffett to almost anyone and they will automatically think "value."

If we are to become as astute as Mr. Buffett, we must learn to think like him. To learn to think as he does, it is imperative to have a sound understanding of the basic principles of value as they apply to real estate. The most common method of determining the value of a particular piece of property is by having an *appraisal* done on it. An *appraisal* is an estimate of an object's worth or value. An appraisal can be used to derive the value of many types of property. Some of these include personal property, such as furnishings, jewelry, and equipment, or real property, such as land, single-family houses, or office buildings.

Appraisals are conducted by individuals specially trained in the principles of property valuation. Appraisers are said to render professional opinions regarding the value of real property that are used in turn by various parties related to a transaction as impartial judgments of the value of the respective properties. Parties interested in obtaining an appraisal include both buyers and sellers of property, as well as third parties such as banks and other lending institutions. In *Income Property Valuation* (Massachusetts: Heath Lexington Books, 1971) author William N. Kinnard describes the five most important elements an appraisal should contain in the following excerpt.

A professional appraisal report should contain as a minimum (1) the identity and legal description of the real estate; (2) the type of value being estimated; (3) the interests being appraised; (4)

the market conditions or decision standards in terms of which the value estimate is made (frequently identified by specifying an "as of" date or effective date for the appraisal); and (5) the value estimate itself.

In addition to the elements described by Kinnard, appraisers should also describe the rationale and methodology from which the value was derived. For example, the appraiser should clearly state what type of appraisal method was used and why it was used. If the appraisal conducted was used to derive the value of a single-family house, the most appropriate appraisal method is the sales comparison method. On the other hand, if the appraisal conducted was used to derive the value of a commercial office building, then the report should be heavily weighted or influenced by the income capitalization method (discussed later in this chapter). The appraiser should also include any facts that may have either a positive or a negative impact on the subject property's value. For example, if a vacant tract of land has current zoning for single-family houses to be built on it, and the tract happens to be situated directly adjacent to the city refuse facility (also known as the "city dump"), this would have an adverse impact on the value of the land and should be clearly stated as such. I know one builder here in our community who purchased just such a tract. The site will accommodate the construction of about 20 houses or so, but happens to back up to the city dump. I couldn't believe my eyes when I saw the first few spec houses go up and thought to myself, "Why would anyone ever want to live there?" Those first few spec houses sat empty for about two years. Since then, several have been sold. But they sure got off to a slow start. My guess is that the builder eventually had to lower the selling price of the houses significantly just to get buyers into them. The builder would have had to pay me to live there, and even then I doubt if it would be worth it.

As Kinnard explains in his book, the process for appraising real property is well defined and specific. Although the appraisal process is an objective and well-defined process, property values nevertheless vary widely. Real estate values are affected by a variety of forces including

Supply and demand issues
The current interest rate environment
Local and national economic conditions
The desirability of the location
School districts
Proximity to shopping
Differences in tax rates

With so many factors impacting value, the same appraisal standards applied to a particular piece of real property in one region may yield entirely different results for a similar piece of real property in another region. These values can furthermore vary widely in the same region, the same town, and even in the same neighborhood.

To further understand the notion of *value*, the notion of *price* must also be considered. While the two terms are similar in meaning, they are not the same. An appraisal serves as an estimate of value only and provides no indication of the price that will actually be paid. For example, an individual shopping for a new appliance such as a range will first determine all the desired features she must have and then begin to shop for one matching these requirements. Once a model is selected, she will then most likely shop around at several locations to determine which store is offering the best price. By purchasing the range at the lowest price available, not only is she able to save money, but she is also said to have received the best value. So while two identical appliances at two different locations may have the same suggested resell price, because one is sold for less money, its equivalent value is actually greater than the one that is priced higher.

While an appraisal provides the basis for price, buyers and sellers in a free market have the ability to negotiate. Kinnard maintains that, "In the perfect market of economic theory, informed and rational buyers would pay no more, and informed and rational sellers would accept no less, than the present worth of the anticipated future benefits from ownership of an asset." Because buyers and sellers are free to negotiate, however, the actual price paid may be, and usually is, different from the stated value in an appraisal report. Price is therefore a reflection of the past. It is what has already occurred. Value, on the other hand, reflects the price that should be paid "in the perfect market of economic theory." Value is therefore a forecast of price and is what *may* occur at some point in the future. Price, on the other hand, is what *has* already occurred at some point in the past.

The Relativity of Value

Before a real estate investor can determine the worth of a particular tract of land, house, or apartment building, he or she must first understand this very important precept, that value is relative. One of my company's primary business activities is to buy and sell single-family houses that are in disrepair and in need of much attention by way of improvements. I typically buy houses in several neighborhoods where home prices average from about $50,000 to $100,000. Before purchasing a house, I have to know three things. First, I must know the sales price of the house. In other words, how much does it cost? Second, I must be able to estimate with a high degree of accuracy the cost of the improvements plus any related transaction costs and carrying costs such as interest and taxes. Finally, I must know what the value of the house will be after all of the improvements have been completed and what price I will be able to sell it for. It is this third component that is extremely location sensitive. For example, the resell value of a 1,000-square-foot house might be $62,000 in the 2400 block of a particular street, but only $32,000 in the 1400 block of the same street. If I rely on comparable sales from the 2400 block to purchase and resell a house located in the 1400 block, I'll never be able to recoup my investment. In *101 Cost Effective Ways to Improve the Value of Your Home* (Chicago: Dearborn Trade, 2004), I wrote about the notion of value as follows:

Although the value or worth of a house or an improvement can be quantified in terms of dollars, it is difficult to do so for two reasons. First, the concept of value is relative. For example, a house that is worth $100,000 in one neighborhood may be worth $125,000 in another neighborhood only two miles away. These differences in value may be due to supply and demand issues, desirability of location, differences in tax rates, or any other number of reasons. Second, although property values can be quantified, there is a degree of subjectivity in doing so.

For instance, two different appraisers who appraise the exact same house will more than likely come up with two different values. This is due in part to the selection process of comparable houses that have sold in the subject property's surrounding neighborhood. While one appraiser may select what he believes to be the three of four most appropriate comparable sales, the other appraiser may select three or four entirely different comparable sales. Since each appraiser has used different comparable sales to derive a value for the subject property, the two values for the same house are almost certain to be different. So although there is a high degree of objectivity in the appraisal process which necessitates that appraisers follow the same standard guidelines, there is also a varying degree of subjectivity which is likely to result in differences in values.

Remember that the appraisal process is not an exact science and that the professional opinion of value rendered by an appraiser is exactly that—an opinion. Property values vary widely from region to region, city to city, and even neighborhood to neighborhood for a host of reasons. For example, while some older communities suffer from functional or economic obsolescence, other newer communities are rapidly growing. Climate plays an especially important role in differences in housing. An in-ground swimming pool, for instance, may be considered essential to many buyers in Florida. In Alaska, however, an in-ground pool would be considered an absolute waste of money. While a swimming pool in Florida adds to the value of property, it would most likely detract from the value of property in Alaska. The only way it would be worth anything is if it were an indoor, heated pool that could be used year round.

In your search for undervalued properties, you should keep this principle in the forefront of your mind at all times. You must always remember the simple, yet ever important principle, that *value is relative*. The relativity of value principle was further explored in *The Complete Guide to Real Estate Finance* (Hoboken, New Jersey: John Wiley & Sons, 2004).

Like many of you, in my earlier years, I owned and managed rental properties and read just about every new real estate book that came out. They all seemed to be saying the same thing with only slight variations in theme, some delving into "nothing down" techniques while others focused on slowly accumulating a portfolio of properties so as to eventually build a level of cash flow sufficient to live off of, otherwise known as the "buy and hold" approach.

The more I read, the more I discovered that none of these books focused on what matters most in real estate, that being the accumulation of properties which are *properly valued*, as well as their subsequent disposition, with the difference being sufficient enough to allow investors the opportunity to profit. Proponents of the buy-and-hold strategy would argue that because the holding period extends over many years, price doesn't matter as long as an investor can purchase real estate with favorable enough terms. Nothing could be further from the truth. It is precisely this kind of misinformation that led thousands, if not millions, of investors over the cliff in the collapse of the stock market in the three-year period that began in the year 2000.

Price didn't matter as long as it was going up and the terms were good. Since value is a function of the price paid and price didn't matter, value didn't matter either. Investors overextended themselves buying on margin and other forms of borrowed funds with absolutely no regard for an asset's value. Most of these investors probably had no conceptual basis for their purchase decisions to begin with. In the end, many of those same investors watched in horror as their life savings evaporated right before their very eyes.

By now I think you are starting to get the picture. Whether you're buying a gallon of milk, a new car, shares of a company's stock, or real estate, the law of the relativity of value cannot be taken lightly. This law is so important, in fact, that every investor's success or failure depends upon obeying it. If the relativity of value as it applies to real estate is disregarded, the fate of investors buying it will be no different than the tens of thousands of those who lost their life savings in the stock market. Try to get in the habit of thinking like the value king, Warren Buffett. You can rest assured that the principle of value is always foremost in his mind, regardless of the type of asset he may be investing in.

Primary Valuation Methods

The three most common methods used by appraisers for determining the value of real estate are the replacement cost method, the income capitalization method, and the sales comparison method. Each appraisal method has its place and serves a unique function in assessing the value of real estate. Commercial properties such as retail centers, office buildings, and apartment complexes, for example, rely primarily on the income method while single-family houses typically rely on the sales comparison method. Since the focus of this book is single-family houses, the appraisal method of most importance to you is the sales comparison method. (See Figure 2.1.)

The Three Most Common Appraisal Methods

1. Replacement Cost Method
2. Income Capitalization Method
3. Sales Comparison Method

Figure 2.1

Replacement Cost Method

The *replacement cost method,* or cost approach, is typically used for estimating the replacement value of physical assets, such as a house or a building, for insurance purposes. For example, if a house were destroyed in a fire or flood, the company providing the insurance coverage would want to know what the actual cost to replace it was. The income method and the sales comparison method are of little or no consequence in estimating replacement costs and would therefore not be applicable to the replacement cost method. The insurance policy you have on your personal residence most likely includes a replacement cost policy with built-in premium adjustments that automatically increase each year due to rises in labor and material costs. While an adjustment is made for rising labor and material costs, adjustments may also be made for depreciation due to wear and aging. For example, a roof that is only 1 year old would certainly have more value than a roof that is 20 years old. The underlying rationale of the replacement cost method is that an informed buyer would not be willing to pay more for a particular house than the cost of building an identical house on a comparable lot in a similar neighborhood.

Income Capitalization Method

The second leading appraisal method is the *income capitalization method*. This method is used to value income-producing property and is used mainly for investment purposes. In *Income Property Valuation*, author Kinnard describes the process of capitalization as follows:

> Real estate is a capital good. This means that the benefits from owning it—whether in the form of money income or amenities, or both—are received over a prolonged period of time. Operationally, this means more than one year; in fact, it is typically for 10, 20, 40, or more years.
>
> In all economic and investment analysis, of which real estate appraisal is an integral part, the value of a capital good is established and measured by calculating the *present worth*, as of a particular valuation date, of the anticipated future benefits, (income) to the owner over a specified time period. The process of converting an income stream into a single value is known as *capitalization*. The result of the capitalization process is a present worth estimate. This is the amount of capital sum that a prudent, typically informed purchaser-investor would pay as of the valuation date for the right to receive the forecast net income over the period specified.

Kinnard's concise description of capitalizing an asset clarifies the process and is so profound that it bears repeating. He states, "The process of converting an income stream into a single value is known as *capitalization*." The income capitalization method then is appropriately used to value buildings such as mini storage units, industrial buildings, mobile home parks, and multifamily apartment buildings. The capitalized value from income-producing real estate is derived directly from the net cash flow, or income, generated by the asset. Investors compare the rates of return earned from various types of assets balanced against the perceived risks and invest their capital accordingly. Assuming that risk is held constant, an investor's return on capital is the same regardless of whether it is derived from real estate, stocks, or bonds. In summary then, the present value of a capital asset is directly related to its future net operating income.

Sales Comparison Method

The appraisal method most appropriate for locating and identifying undervalued properties such as single-family houses is the *sales comparison method*. The sales comparison method is by far the most commonly used appraisal method of the three approaches. This is due in large part to the fact that the number of single-family dwellings is much greater than any other type of property. This method is based on the premise that the price paid for recent sales of similar properties represents the price buyers are willing to pay and is therefore representative of true market value. The price paid for like properties may vary for any number of reasons. For example, changes in interest rates, changes in unemployment rates, changes in general economic conditions, as well as changes in the cost of materials and land. The combination of these different factors may or may not affect the equilibrium for the supply and demand of available properties.

The sales comparison method is based upon the premise of substitution and maintains that a buyer would not pay any more for real property than the cost of purchasing an equally desirable substitute in its respective market. This method also assumes that all comparable sales used in the appraisal process are legitimate arm's length transactions. The sales comparison method furthermore provides that comparable sales used have occurred under normal market conditions. For example, this assumption would exclude properties bought and sold under foreclosure conditions or those purchased from a bank's real estate owned, or REO, portfolio.

The sales comparison method typically examines three or more properties that are similar to one another. The values of the properties are then adjusted based upon similarities and differences among them.

For example, if the subject property had a two-car garage while the comparable property had a three-car garage, an adjustment would be made for the difference to bring the values in line with each other. In this case, the comparable property's value would be adjusted downward to compensate for the additional garage unit. In other words, the value of the additional garage unit is subtracted so as to make it the equivalent of a two-car garage.

In your search for undervalued single-family houses, the sales comparison method of appraising real property is the most appropriate choice. Most real estate agents will provide you with comparable sales, or *comps* as they are also known, free of charge. Agents provide this invaluable service to clients in the hope that they can help them find a house they want to buy and ultimately earn a commission. The data is accessible to licensed real estate agents through the Multiple Listing Service, or MLS. Agents can do a search in the MLS using any number of search criteria and can easily pull up active sales (those houses currently listed and available for sale), as well as houses that have already sold. You can then take this data and use it to compare to the house you are thinking about purchasing. You should be objective when comparing comps to your subject property so as to assess its value as accurately as possible. I recommend actually driving by the houses you are using as comps to look at their overall condition and make notes as you do. After looking at 15 or 20 houses in an afternoon, they all start to look the same. It's easy to forget which house had what features. As you become more and more familiar with a particular neighborhood, it will no longer be necessary to drive out and look at all the comps because you will already have a firsthand knowledge of property values in that area. Then when you are alerted to an opportunity, you will already know how its value compares relative to the other houses in the same area. This level of familiarity with property values takes time, so don't get discouraged after your first time out looking at houses. If you are going to be successful in acquiring undervalued properties, you have to be prepared to put in the time required to become an expert in your area.

To summarize, each of the three chief appraisal methods serves a unique function by estimating value using a different approach. Depending on the type of property that is being evaluated, all three methods may be taken into consideration, each with their respective weights applied to the value as deemed appropriate. The appraisal process is then completed by a reconciliation of the three methods, which in turn lends consideration to the type and reliability of the market data used, the applicability of each method to the type of property appraised, and the type of value sought. In the pursuit of undervalued single-family houses, the sales comparison method of estimating value is the most appropriate choice.

PART 2

How to Find Undervalued Properties

3

Six Conventional Methods of Finding Undervalued Properties

In Part 1, we examined some of the issues fundamental to understanding value. It only stands to reason that before you can purchase undervalued houses, you must first have a firm grasp on the concept of value. We also determined that of the three most commonly used appraisal methods, the sales comparison method is the most appropriate choice for purchasing single-family houses. The sales comparison method is similar to shopping for a new appliance, a new purse, or a new set of tools. Before purchasing any of these items, you are first likely to examine items of similar quality, style, and design at a variety of stores. After determining which item best fits your needs and provides the best value, the decision to purchase is made. Although we are all guilty of impulse shopping from time to time, the decision to purchase impulsively is not really made without any basis of fact. In other words, even though you may buy an item that you had no intention of buying when coming into a store, because you have seen items similar in price and quality, you are able to recognize the impulse item as a bargain.

Buying houses based on this same premise is no different than buying miscellaneous goods at the local discount store. Because you have seen literally hundreds of houses of similar quality and design, you are now capable of recognizing a bargain when you see one. My company, Symphony Homes, is involved in many aspects of the real estate business (see Afterword). While our core business is the construction of new residential condominiums and single-family houses, a related business is the purchase of preowned houses that are typically in varying degrees of disrepair. The houses are purchased, then rehabbed and refurbished to like-new condition, and then quickly sold at a price slightly above market. We are currently averaging about one house per week, but are in the process of accelerating our operations to two houses a week. To achieve this level of buying and selling, the Symphony Homes team must be acutely aware of local market values and be able to recognize an undervalued property instantly. When an opportunity shows up on our radar screen that warrants leaving the office to look at it, we can quickly assess whether or not the subject property meets our investment criteria. The key to this process is having a steady flow of opportunities sent to us automatically. Part 2 of this book includes numerous ways you can find undervalued properties that are available for sale. Some of these methods may require more effort than others, but all of them are devised to enable you to turn your dreams into a finely tuned real estate money machine. By establishing a systematic approach to finding undervalued properties, you'll discover that there are more opportunities than you have time or money to invest in.

Included in Figure 3.1 are six conventional methods you can begin using right now to find undervalued houses. You can choose to use as

**Six Conventional Methods for
Finding Undervalued Properties**

1. Professional associations
2. Classified advertisements
3. Real estate publications
4. Internet Web sites
5. Real estate investment clubs
6. Tax exchange networks

Figure 3.1

few as one or two of the suggested methods or to use all of them. The more of these methods that are used, the more opportunities you will have. I recommend starting out by experimenting with several of the methods you are most familiar with. As you gain more experience and are eventually able to devote yourself full time to the real estate business, I suggest using all of them. The more undervalued properties you have to review and analyze, the better and more profitable your chances will become.

Professional Associations

There are a variety of industry related professionals who can alert you to potential investment opportunities. These consist of people who deal with various facets of the real estate industry in one form or another and include professionals such as real estate appraisers, mortgage brokers, title insurance closing agents and title processors, property insurance agents, property surveyors, and engineers, to name a few. I recommend getting to know as many of these individuals as possible. Like the real estate agents, the more people you have on your team scouting for undervalued properties, the greater your chances of success will be. Although you will come to know many of these professionals through the normal course of business, I suggest taking a more proactive approach by calling them to introduce yourself, then stopping by for a personal introduction, and finally by mailing them a thank you card as well as periodic reminders of the business you are in. The bottom line here is to do whatever it takes to keep your name in front of them so you will be the first one they think of when they happen to come across the type of property you are looking for.

Of the group of professionals listed here, real estate appraisers are one of the best sources for finding undervalued real estate deals. Appraisers are in the business of studying and analyzing real estate market data every day. Their profession necessitates the ongoing comparison of like properties that is fundamental to the appraisal process. The value for the subject property for which the appraisal is being conducted is derived by comparing it to similar properties with similar characteristics and in similar neighborhoods. Although appraisers use properties that have already sold for comparison purposes, they nevertheless review active listings (properties that have not yet sold) that can also provide valuable information. The longer an appraiser studies a particular market, the more familiar she becomes with property values in that area and the more capable she is of recognizing potential investment opportunities. An appraiser acting as a scout or bird dog would be compensated differently than a real estate agent would. While real estate agents are paid on a commission basis for only those properties that you purchase, appraisers should be compensated on a fee basis for properties that you purchase. A typical finder's fee may range anywhere from $250 to as much as $500 or more. I prefer to reward appraisers based on the spread between a property's actual sale price and its potential resale price. In other words, the more money that's in a deal, the more I can afford to pay. If I can only make $10,000 on a deal, I can justify a payment of $250 if I decide to take it. On the other hand, if I can make $20,000 on a deal, that deal is worth more to me and I justify a higher fee of $500 if I decide to take it. Like the real estate agents you are working with, be sure to honor your commitment to pay the appraisers a finder's fee for properties you purchase, especially if you expect them to continue bringing you potential opportunities.

Although you may at first be concerned about the possibility that one of these professionals will locate an undervalued property and then "steal it" from you by keeping it for themselves, let me assure you that, in most cases, your fears are unfounded. You may be thinking, "Why don't they buy the house themselves if it's such a good deal?" That is certainly a valid question and one that deserves an answer. I used to ask myself that same question. Over the years, however, I have come to learn that even though these groups of people are professionals who work in the real estate industry on a daily basis, most of them share the same fears as those who work outside the real estate industry. In other words, they are not comfortable on a personal level assuming the risk that is inherent in real estate. That demon we call *fear* exists in the minds of many people and prevents them from taking action. This demon is also a master of deceit and labors tirelessly and endlessly to cloud our minds with "what-ifs" to convince us that we cannot possibly succeed. It is up to us to raise the shield of *courage*, and then wield the sword of *truth* and slay the demon. If this demon exists in your mind, I promise you that you have the power to smite him into oblivion. It is up to you, however, to pick up the sword and use it. Knowledge will supplant fear, courage will take root, and truth will surely prevail.

I work directly with several individuals on a daily basis who have not learned to conquer their fears. One such individual is a real estate agent who is constantly on the lookout for undervalued properties for me. I mentioned rather jokingly to her recently that if I wasn't careful, she would stop sending deals to me and start keeping them for herself.

She responded by telling me, "Oh, you don't have to worry about that. I'm not cut out to be a real estate investor. It's too risky for me." Well, imagine that. Here's a lady who spends several hours a week searching for bargain-priced houses for one of her best clients while stating that investing in real estate is too risky. Where is the disconnect? She clearly understands the concept of value, and she clearly recognizes an undervalued property when she sees one. She furthermore has direct evidence that buying these properties and reselling them is indeed a sound and profitable strategy. The disconnect lies within her own mind. Somewhere along the way, a little bit at a time, my friend allowed the fears that come with minor setbacks to overcome her. Each time she succumbs to one of these setbacks, another link in the chain of fear is formed. Each time another link is formed, the chain becomes stronger and therefore more difficult to break until, finally, it is almost impossible to escape. The only way to set herself free is to remove the obstacles that exist within her own mind. In order for that to happen, she must draw upon the powers of courage and faith and make a concerted effort to alter her behavioral patterns that have formed over the course of her life. The strength gained from these initial actions will enable her to set a new course in life, one guided by courage rather than one driven by fear.

Classified Ads

Classified advertisements in smaller, local newspapers are another great way to find undervalued properties. Almost all newspapers feature a real estate classified ads section for single-family houses and other types of properties that are available for sale. Many of these ads are placed by real estate agents and are designed to prompt you to call their offices. Look for ads that use key words like *investment opportunity* or *handyman special*. This kind of descriptive language is usually indicative of older houses in established neighborhoods that may appeal to investors and are generally worth taking the time to call on. Even if it turns out that the house is no longer available or does not meet your investment objectives, it still provides an opportunity for you to create a dialogue with a real estate agent who may be able to assist you in the search for similar properties.

Many of the ads listed in the classified section are for sale by owners, also known as FSBOs. Once again, look for key words that may indicate the owner is anxious to sell, can offer flexible terms, or has a house that may be offered at a price below retail. As you become more familiar with prices in your local market, you will increase your ability to recognize a good deal when you see one. Although some FSBO sellers are able to assess accurately the proper sale price for their houses, many are not aware of what the true value really is. For instance, if a homeowner has lived in the same house for 20 or 30 years, he or she may not realize that home prices have increased to the extent that they have and may very well be selling the house well below market. While sellers may be trying to save money by selling a house on their own to save the commission expense, their shortsighted approach may cost them in the long run because of a lack of knowledge with respect to local market prices. Their willingness to forgo a true market value selling price, however, can potentially result in an excellent opportunity for you.

Finally, rather than limiting yourself only to ads that others are placing, you also can easily place your own ad in a classified section such as "real estate wanted." You don't need to spend much money on these ads. A well-written ad can be just as effective as a larger, more expensive ad. Your goal is to get people who are motivated and want to sell their houses to call you. If the sellers are in a distressed situation such as a pending foreclosure, or perhaps a divorce, they have every reason to call. In situations such as these, sellers are not usually thinking about making any money from the transaction. Instead, they are just trying to salvage their credit or relieve the tension and pressure caused by their distressed circumstances. In addition to running an ad in the classified section of the newspaper, you may also want to consider running a small, inexpensive display ad such as the ones illustrated here.

Although a display ad will cost a little more than a classified ad, the heightened visibility of it should generate more telephone calls for you and, therefore, increase your opportunities for success. You may also want to consider using a telephone number in the ad that directs sellers to a prerecorded message that further explains what you have to offer by outlining some of the basic terms and conditions that you are offering. This prerecorded message helps to more effectively prequalify those sellers who are genuinely interested in selling their houses and helps to reduce the time you spend on the telephone with tire kickers and curiosity seekers.

Real Estate Publications

There are a number of publications that specialize in advertising both residential and commercial real estate. It is quite common to find magazine racks stocked with a variety of real estate magazines in almost every town and city across the country. These publications are typically placed at local real estate offices, grocery stores, banks, mortgage offices, insurance agencies, attorneys' offices, appraisal firms, and surveying companies, to name a few. Believe it or not, these publications can be an excellent source for finding undervalued properties. Although it is true that the majority of listings are the everyday run-of-the-mill advertisements featuring single-family houses at full retail price, it has been my experience that there are usually at least a few brokers or agents who specialize in wholesale opportunities. Agents specializing in bargain-priced real estate deals generally represent one or more lenders attempting to dispose of nonperforming assets such as their bank's real estate owned, or REO, portfolio. These are properties that have been foreclosed on and taken back by the lending institution originating the loan. Lenders work through a network of preferred real estate agents whose primary activities generally center around wholesaling properties to investors. Because the agents have their own network of investors whom they conduct business with regularly, the disposition of these nonperforming assets is greatly facilitated. Lenders like this arrangement because they know they have a contact at the local level to sell their properties. Brokers and sales agents like this arrangement because they have a steady flow of listings to sell, as well as a pool of investors to sell them to. And finally, investors like this arrangement because they can purchase single-family houses and other types of real estate at below market value.

Real estate publications such as the magazines mentioned here can be an important source for finding undervalued properties. Don't underestimate their importance by overlooking this important resource. Some of my best deals have come from agents who advertise in this type of magazine. My relationship with one of them in particular has developed to the point to where he will actually call me immediately upon listing a foreclosure that meets my investment criteria because he knows that I have the ability, as well as the intention, of following through with an offer to purchase if I like the deal. His willingness to alert me to such opportunities enables our company to act quickly in purchasing these types of properties. In fact, I recently closed on one such property. The lender's original selling price was $22,500, a price I would gladly have paid if required; however, we were able to negotiate down to an even $20,000. The house will require approximately $15,000 in repairs, carrying costs, and transaction costs to bring it up to a like-new condition. Comparable sales market data suggests a resale price of $65,000, which will net us a tidy $30,000 or so in profit. Therein lies the power of the various types of real estate magazines that can be found all across the nation.

Internet Resources

The Internet is a terrific tool for finding all kinds of information on undervalued real estate. By using a major search engine like Google or Yahoo!, you can type in a search string such as "bargain real estate," or "cheap houses," or "foreclosures." You will also, of course, want to include the area or region in which you are looking for undervalued properties. For example, if you live in Texas and are looking for bargain-priced houses in Houston, your search string would include something like "cheap houses Houston Texas" or "foreclosures Houston Texas." There are numerous companies that are in the business of providing this type of information, especially that which relates to foreclosed real estate. The information from these services is usually available for a nominal fee and is often billed on a subscriber basis, meaning that the company bills you on an ongoing or recurring periodic basis, such as monthly, until such time as the subscription is canceled. I subscribe to one such service that provides information on foreclosed real estate. The information on the Web site is updated on a daily basis. In addition, e-mail alerts are sent to me automatically every time a new property is listed on the site. The alerts are based on predetermined geographic criteria set by me, so I'm not getting a lot of alerts on properties that I have no interest in. One drawback with these services, however, is that the new listings sometimes lag behind the time when they actually first became available. For example, if a property pops up in one of my e-mail alerts and I decide to call the listing agent on it, there's a chance that it may already be sold. This is certainly not always the case, but you should be aware that it does happen from time to time. That's why it's a good idea to build relationships with as many agents as possible who specialize in selling undervalued properties such as foreclosures for their client, the lender. The more agents there are scouting for bargain-priced properties for you, the better your chances of success will be.

Other good Internet sources include Web sites for smaller local newspapers as well as larger metropolitan newspapers. Most all newspapers now list their entire classified section online. The information is kept current since it is usually updated each day. Furthermore, the paper's archives can be searched for ads from previous dates. Real estate agents are one of the largest users of the classified ads section and often place many of their listings there. A quick perusal of the ads for bargain-priced houses would include looking for terms like *handyman special, investor opportunity*, or *needs work*. Ads such as these are worth taking the time to call the agents on for two reasons. First, the house you are calling on may in fact be a viable undervalued property, and second, it gives you the opportunity to create a dialog with yet another source of real estate agents. If the particular house you called on does not turn out to meet your investment criteria, that's okay. At least now you have established one more contact who can be on the lookout for undervalued properties.

Real Estate Investment Clubs

As the popularity of real estate as an investment continues to grow, so do the number of real estate investment clubs. Whether you live in Los

Angeles, California; Atlanta, Georgia; or somewhere in between, there's a good chance you'll be able to find an investment club in your town or city. Most larger metropolitan areas even have several clubs, so you should be able to find one without too much difficulty. Investment clubs provide a great networking opportunity for getting to know other real estate professionals who share similar interests. Members typically include other real estate investors, brokers and sales agents, tax and real estate attorneys, architectural engineers, land surveyors, appraisers, and anyone else who may share an interest in real estate. Club and association members usually meet on a regular basis, such as monthly, to discuss current events and share information. Many real estate investment clubs also feature guest speakers periodically who share their specialized knowledge on a particular topic. For instance, a club may invite a certified public accountant, or CPA, who specializes in real estate tax law to share tax strategies with investors of rental properties. One way to find real estate associations in your area is by asking some of the sales agents and brokers you already know. You can also do a search on the Internet using a term like "real estate investment clubs." One site I've used is called Real Estate Promo.com and is located at www.real estatepromo.com. Click on the link entitled Investment Clubs to locate a club near you. The site has clubs listed in almost all 50 states, so you should be able to find something near you. Another similar site is offered by a company called Creative Real Estate Online. Their Web site is located at www.real-estate-online.com. Go to the home page and click on Real Estate Clubs to find an investment association in your area.

Tax Exchange Networks

Tax exchanges are popular among investors because they can be used to defer capital gains taxes that would otherwise be due when real estate is sold. Federal law encourages tax exchanges among investors and has established the rules by which investors may do so as contained in Internal Revenue Code Section 1031. IRC Section 1031 provides that the exchange of certain types of property will not result in the recognition of gain or loss: "No gain or loss shall be recognized if property held for productive use in a trade or business or for investment purposes is exchanged solely for property of like-kind." It is important that the requirements of Section 1031 are carefully met so that when an exchange is completed, the tax on the transaction will be deferred as intended. The transaction must be structured in such a manner that it is an exchange of one property for another instead of the sale of one property and the purchase of another. Certain requirements must be met under the Section 1031 exchange rules for a transaction to qualify for tax-deferred treatment. First, tax-deferred exchanges are limited to real property only and do not include personal property. Real property includes property such as single-family houses, land, commercial buildings, and apartment complexes. Personal property includes property such as automobiles, boats, computers, and equipment. Second, the properties being exchanged must be investment or income properties; therefore, your personal residence or a second home such as a vacation home would not qualify. In addition, the replacement property must be "like-kind." In other words, it must also be real property since all real property is considered to be like-kind. Property must also be held for 12 months to qualify for tax-deferred treatment, the same period of time required for long-term capital gains treatment. One requirement that is sometimes difficult for investors to meet is that a replacement property must be identified within 45 days of closing the property they just sold. Finally, sellers must be able to close on the replacement property within 180 days of closing the property they already sold. While the requirements for a Section 1031 tax-deferred exchange mentioned here are by no means exhaustive, they should provide you with insight into how the process works.

Investors often form tax exchange networks or groups to facilitate the sale of property in accordance with the law that governs exchanges. The networks are made up of many individual investors who prefer to delay their tax liability when buying and selling property. The opportunity to find undervalued properties among tax exchange participants arises when investors have no choice but to act quickly because of the time constraints imposed on them under the Section 1031 guidelines. These strict time constraints can impact sellers on both ends of the transaction, meaning the property they are divesting themselves of and also the one they are acquiring. If the seller has not identified a new property to purchase yet, she may not be that motivated and may in fact stall the sale of the property. On the other hand, if the seller has identified another property that must soon be closed because of the expiration of the other seller's time, then she must be prepared to rapidly strike a deal with a buyer of her property. Information about tax exchange groups in your area can be found by searching the Internet using a search string like, "1031 tax exchange network Denver," or "tax exchange groups Arizona."

In this chapter, we examined six conventional methods you can begin using right now to find bargain-priced houses. Professional associations and classified advertisements are all great resources for locating these types of properties. Real estate publications, Web sites, real estate investment clubs, and tax exchange networks are also great resources. The more of these methods you have at your disposal, the better your chances of finding potential investment opportunities will be. Regardless of where you live, there are always an abundance of investment opportunities available, many of which can be found right in your own backyard. You just have to know how to find them. By using a systematic and comprehensive approach, you will be able to locate more undervalued properties than you have time or money to invest in.

4

Distressed Properties Create Undervalued Opportunities

In the last chapter, we studied six conventional methods that can be used to find undervalued properties. These included joining professional associations, searching classified advertisements, using real estate publications, searching Web sites, participating in real estate investment clubs, and exploring opportunities that may be available in tax exchange networks. In this chapter, we'll explore four additional ways to locate undervalued real estate (see Figure 4.1). The houses we'll discuss in this chapter are all properties that are in distress for one reason or another. They include houses that have been abandoned or are vacant, houses suffering from functional or economic obsolescence, or those that have been neglected by their owners. Each of these methods of locating undervalued properties can be added to the set discussed in Chapter 3 to fortify your existing body of knowledge.

Four Ways to Locate Distressed Properties

1. Abandoned houses
2. Functional obsolescence
3. External obsolescence arising from either location or economic forces
4. Neglected houses

Figure 4.1

Abandoned Houses

As you drive through neighborhoods in your search for investment opportunities, be sure to pay special attention to those houses that appear vacant. Vacant houses are more of a liability than an asset for their owners, so they are oftentimes available at bargain prices. The sellers have moved out for any number of reasons and are no longer around to care for the house. It may be that they just went through a divorce, had a new house built, or were transferred to another area. Whatever the reason, the end result is the same. If the owners are to prevent the house from going into foreclosure, they must not only make the payments on their new house, but must also keep up with the payments on the old one. After just a few months of making double house payments, sellers of vacant properties become very motivated. In some cases, they are happy just to get somebody to relieve them of their monthly obligation, regardless of any equity they may have built up in the house.

Obvious signs of empty houses include overgrown weeds and shrubs, newspapers in the driveway, and a general rundown appearance. Sometimes these houses have only recently been vacated, while other times they have been sitting empty for several months. There may be a FSBO (for sale by owner) sign or a real estate firm's sign in the front yard. If so, this makes your job of finding the owner much easier. If there is no sign out front, you may have to do a little research. Usually a telephone call to the local taxing authority can provide you with the information you need. The clerks who work in the tax offices and who are responsible for maintaining the tax roles can quickly and easily provide you with the current owner's name and the address that the tax bill is mailed to. With the name and address, you can call information to obtain a phone number for the owners. If the number is unlisted, you can express your interest in the property through the mail since you at least have the owner's address. Be sure to provide them with your telephone number so that if the owner is interested in selling her house to you, she can contact you with as little effort as possible.

Functional Obsolescence

The term *functional obsolescence* is used to describe property with an impairment of desirability typically arising from its being out of date with respect to design and style, capacity and utility in relation to site, lack of modern facilities, and other such qualities considered to be obsolete or outdated. Differences in characteristics become especially apparent when a property having some degree of functional obsolescence is compared to a similar, but newer and more modern, facility. Property suffering from functional obsolescence is often adversely affected by a loss in property value because buyers are not willing to pay as much for outdated houses or buildings. This is true because, as new designs and technologies emerge, older properties with outdated designs and technologies become less desirable to buyers.

Functional obsolescence presents itself in two primary forms, or types. The first type of functional obsolescence is referred to as a "deficiency." A house having only gas space heaters rather than being equipped with central heating is an example of a functional deficiency.

In this example, the lack of what is commonly considered to be a standard form of heating would have a negative impact on its value, especially if other homes in the area had been modernized with newer central heating equipment. Situations like this can create excellent undervalued purchase opportunities for investors. If a homeowner has neglected to update the heating equipment, there's a good chance the rest of the house may be suffering from functional obsolescence as well. For example, the kitchen may have outdated appliances, cabinets, countertops, and lighting. The bathroom may have an outdated vanity, fixtures, flooring, and shower or bathtub. Houses like this can easily be repaired and renovated and quite often provide investors with excellent upside potential. The ideal situation is to locate a house suffering from functional obsolescence in a neighborhood where most of the rest of the houses have already been updated. The surrounding properties will already have risen in value, creating a perfect environment in which to increase the value of the house that has not yet been updated.

The second type of functional obsolescence is known as a "superadequacy" and refers to property having some design element that may serve no other purpose than to be aesthetically appealing to the viewer. An example of a super-adequacy would be a waterfall created inside an office building that flows into a stream running through the center of the main floor from one end of the building to the other. Although the running water can create a strong visual impact and be very soothing to the viewer, the stream does nothing to generate revenue for the office building. The waterfall and stream, as beautiful as they may be, occupy space that might otherwise be leased to a tenant. The lack of rental income from this space represents a cost to the owner because it is not being used to produce revenue. It can furthermore be argued that the stream detracts from the profitability of the building because of the additional expenses required to operate and maintain it. So, not only does the owner not earn income from the space occupied by the waterfall and stream, but also must pay for the cost of keeping the water clean, the special lighting it requires, and the electricity needed to operate it. Opportunities arise for investors to convert the non-income-producing space into space that generates revenue. Careful analysis is required in buildings having super-adequacies because sometimes amenities like waterfalls and streams or spacious foyers are what attract tenants to the building to begin with. These elements can sometimes be what give the building character and beauty. The unique design features of one building may be what differentiate it from a competitor, making it more desirable and therefore more valuable.

Outdated houses affected by functional deficiencies, such as those in need of repair, are precisely the types of deals I look for in our rehab business. When a potential undervalued investment opportunity that warrants leaving the office is brought to my attention, the first thing I look at as I'm approaching the house is the overall condition of the neighborhood and, more particularly, the area immediately bordering the house. If most of the homes in the area, and especially those closest to the subject property, are clean, well maintained, and generally in good condition, then I'll take time to actually stop and get out to look at the house. On the other hand, if there are old, beat-up cars sitting up on jacks parked in the driveways, boats stored in the front yard, and beer cans in the street, I keep right on driving. There's no point in even stopping to look at a house that is surrounded by other junky houses. Repairs to older houses that need to be updated and renovated are usually not that difficult to make or to have done. If you're not the handyman type, there are subcontractors for just about anything you need done. It goes without saying that it is important to factor in the costs for both labor and materials when analyzing property suffering from functional obsolescence in order to properly evaluate its expected level of profitability.

External Obsolescence

The term *external obsolescence* is used to describe factors outside of the property, where the impairment of desirability arises from either location or economic forces and typically has an adverse impact on the value of the property. *Location obsolescence* occurs when legislative enactments that restrict or impair property rights, such as changes in zoning ordinances, are made and are inconsistent with the immediate area and consequently affect the optimum use of the land. Location obsolescence also can occur when newly developed land is incompatible with the properties surrounding it. For example, the peace and quiet that is generally found in a particular residential neighborhood can easily be disrupted by the approval of a zoning change that will bring in new shopping centers. The increase in traffic to the new commercial site will likely have a negative affect on the once placid community. While living in Texas, I saw this firsthand as a new national discount store had just won approval to be built next to a once-private community. Many of the local residents opposed the construction of the discount store, but in the end, the national retailer won out. This resulted in a significant increase in traffic, bringing thousands of new shoppers into the area. And this was only the beginning. The new discount store, now an anchor in the community, opened the door for the approval of other giant retailers, grocery stores, and shopping centers. Families choosing to live in the existing neighborhood adjacent to all of the new shopping centers now have to contend with increases in traffic, noise, automobile exhaust, and traffic lights, all of which detract from the desirability of living there. While the additional tax revenues generated by the newly developed commercial businesses are beneficial to the local city government, this is of little comfort to the residents living there.

The term *economic obsolescence* is used to describe property with an impairment of desirability or useful life arising from economic forces and changes in supply and demand relationships. The most common causes of economic obsolescence are changes in general economic conditions, such as a rise in interest rates, a reduction in demand for goods and services, increased foreign competition, changes in governmental regulations, available supply of energy, and the availability and cost of raw materials. Because external obsolescence usually has a negative effect on earnings, the loss in property value is derived from the loss in income. As an area affected by external obsolescence experiences a reduction in property values, a spillover effect may impact the surrounding neighborhood, causing it to deteriorate also. As the demand for housing in a languishing neighborhood declines, there is often a corresponding increase in the rate of crime.

Finally, external obsolescence is described as a loss in property value resulting from changes in the surrounding neighborhood or community. For instance, the value of a house would be adversely affected if it were located in a neighborhood that had experienced a significant increase in crime. An increase in traffic and noise levels may also contribute to a decline in value.

So the question naturally arises, where are the opportunities to buy undervalued property in a neighborhood that is declining in value and increasing in crime? The answer lies in an investor's ability to perceive positive changes in this type of community that represent the initial stages of a turnaround situation. In *The Complete Guide to Buying and Selling Apartment Buildings* (Hoboken, New Jersey: John Wiley & Sons, 2005), I wrote about similar conditions that have the potential to represent excellent buying opportunities for the watchful and astute investor.

The migration in and out of neighborhoods is sometimes cyclical in nature, with the cycles lasting many years, perhaps even decades. An example of this is what has occurred in many larger cities over the last 100 years or so. In their infancy, homes sprang up all around the city. As these cities began to grow and mature, many people left the inner city areas and moved to the surrounding suburbs. The decline in demand for inner-city areas led to lower rents and ultimately deteriorating conditions in many cases. The growth in suburban America created a whole new set of problems, most of them related to heavy traffic conditions. In an effort to avoid these lengthy daily commutes, we have seen in recent years a return of younger couples, as well as singles, to the inner-city area. Neighborhoods that only a few years ago attracted only low-income families now find themselves in vogue and have undergone a dramatic transformation. In many cases, older buildings have been completely razed and replaced with new, upscale apartments that attract affluent professionals who work in the downtown area. Simply put, it is critical to note the trends that are occurring in the community you are considering putting your investment capital to work in. Acquiring a Class C apartment complex in a neighborhood that has reversed trend and is enjoying an increase in popularity and demand may very well prove to be a perfect value play opportunity.

Although this example cites value play opportunities for apartment owners, the same principle applies to those investors desiring to purchase other types of property, such as single-family houses. The key to taking advantage of buying opportunities like this is to detect the positive changes that occur in the early stages of a community's transformation. That doesn't mean you have to be the first one buying in a neighborhood where you perceive a change is about to occur. You should instead act prudently by waiting for signs of life such as other larger investors or developers who are making a serious financial commitment to the area you are considering. These larger players work in concert with banks and financial institutions that use market studies supported by empirical evidence to back their decisions. Once their projects prove to be successful, then it's time to jump on the bandwagon! Houses in older neighborhoods that are experiencing a revitalization can be renovated, updated, and modernized to make them more appealing to the types of upscale buyers who are likely to be moving into the area. If you wait too long to begin buying properties, the increase in demand will push up prices making it more difficult to profit. On the other hand, if you can catch the investment wave in the early stages of the turnaround while many of the property values are still depressed, you can significantly increase your chances of success. An alternative strategy is to purchase as many properties as you can in the early stages of a turnaround and hold them in your investment portfolio as rentals. Then as the market really begins to heat up and demand is accelerating, you can begin renovating and modernizing the houses to sell them for maximum profit.

Neglected Properties

Owners of real estate sometimes tend to neglect their property for one reason or another. In one recent example, I purchased just such a house. The owner of the property had owned the house for many years and had rented it to his son. The son eventually got married and moved out. The dad continued to rent the property for a while, but after his most recent tenant moved, he decided to sell. The dad, however, made the mistake of not reading *101 Cost Effective Ways to Increase the Value of Your Home* (Chicago: Dearborn Trade, 2004) written by none other than yours truly. The book offers advice based on many years of personal experience on the most cost-effective ways to improve a house. Some of these include commonsense approaches such as performing a thorough cleanup of the exterior, pruning overgrown shade trees, and painting the exterior of the house. A recurring theme used throughout the book is that *visibility adds value*.

It helps to know from a resale standpoint where you will be able to get the greatest "bang for the buck" on various types of home improvements that are made. For example, while spending $7,500 on a foundation repair may be required to get a house sold, the repair itself is not very visible and does nothing to improve the appearance of a house. On the other hand, spending the same $7,500 on sprucing up the landscaping, installing new flooring in the kitchen and baths, and perhaps painting the interior of the house has a potentially much greater return for the same amount of dollars invested. This is due to the fact that these improvements are all highly visible and can greatly enhance the beauty of the home. People tend to buy what they "see." In general, repairs and modifications that have a greater propensity to improve the aesthetics of a home will realize a greater return for an equal amount of money spent on a repair that does nothing to improve a house's appearance.

Because only a minimum amount of repair work had been done before listing the house for sale, it did not show very well. One of the biggest problems was its curb appeal. Instead of looking bright and cheery on the outside, it looked dark and dreary. The dark-colored paint that had been used on the exterior, along with trees that needed pruning and overgrown grass and bushes, all combined to make the house appear uninviting from the outside. When prospective buyers are previewing homes, they usually have at least 8 to 10 homes on their list to look at. If the house is not appealing from the outside, buyers oftentimes won't even bother to stop to look at the inside of it. They simply check it off their list and drive on to the next house. As a result of the house's poor curb appeal, it sat on the market for close to a year with very little showing activity. The longer it sat on the market, the more anxious the owner became to sell it. The house was originally listed for sale at a price of $54,000, but had been reduced to $45,000.

Knowing the history of the property, I called the listing sales agent to make an offer. I explained to the sales agent that as an investor, I look at numerous properties every week and that his listing was merely one of many. This being the case, I told him that I was willing to make an all-cash offer of $38,000, that the offer would be a one-time offer, and that the seller had until noon the following day to respond. My purpose for doing this was to let the seller know that I was a serious and qualified buyer and that I was not interested in going back and forth in an ongoing negotiating process. In addition, I wanted to place a fairly short fuse on the offer to force a timely response. The listing agent wrote the offer up and presented it to the seller that afternoon. The next day, shortly after noon, he contacted me to inform me that the seller had accepted my offer. Subsequent to his acceptance, I closed on the property within 30 days. My crews are working on the house now to prepare it for resell. Exterior improvements to the house will include painting the outside a lighter and brighter color, a general cleanup of the grounds, and making landscaping improvements such as mowing and pruning. Interior improvements will include painting the interior, replacing all of the flooring, replacing the light fixtures, and making a few miscellaneous repairs. The estimate for the repairs is approximately $8,500. Once all of the improvements have been completed, the house will be placed back on the market and will be listed at a sales price of $64,900. After transaction and carrying costs, our company should net approximately $15,000 on this property.

This illustration represents a classic example of a house that had been neglected by its owner. The owner's failure to properly care for the house eventually resulted in having to sell it at a greatly reduced price, which in turn created an opportunity for an investor such as myself. Although it is true that the owner could have made the needed improvements and sold the property for full market value himself, for whatever reason he elected not to and was apparently content to accept the offer tendered to him.

In this chapter, we studied four additional ways to locate undervalued real estate. The methods discussed in this chapter pertained to properties that are in distress for one reason or another. They included houses that have been abandoned or are vacant, houses suffering from functional or economic obsolescence, and those that have been neglected by their owners for one reason or another. Keep the methods discussed in this chapter in mind as you search for undervalued properties and you'll discover firsthand just how effective they can be.

5

How You Can Help Distressed Sellers by Purchasing Their Undervalued Properties

In the last chapter, we explored four methods for locating undervalued properties that pertained to distressed houses. They included finding houses that had been abandoned or were vacant for one reason or another, houses that were suffering from functional or economic obsolescence, and those that had been neglected by their owners. In this chapter, we'll examine the various situations that cause sellers to become distressed and the effects these circumstances have on the property they own. Homeowners may experience any number of life-changing events that can have a significant impact on many aspects of their lives. Some of these include a job transfer, a divorce, the loss of employment by one or both spouses, filing for personal bankruptcy, reaching the golden years and settling into a life of retirement, and, finally, the death or serious illness of a family member or other loved one (see Figure 5.1). Although some people may feel that buying houses from sellers in distressed circumstances borders on taking unfair advantage of them, I would contend that just the opposite is true. If anyone needs help disposing of their real estate, it is owners of property who are undergoing difficult circumstances for one reason or another. Getting rid of an unwanted house becomes secondary to these life-changing events. By purchasing houses from distressed sellers, you are actually helping them by relieving what can be a tremendous source of stress for them. In most cases, for example, a seller who is going through a life-changing event such as the loss of a job or a divorce is all too glad to be relieved of a huge debt obligation such as a mortgage. In reality, selling a house becomes secondary to a more immediate and fundamental need that has arisen due to what are often unforeseen circumstances. By pur-

Seven Causes of Seller Distress

1. Transfer or relocation
2. Divorce
3. Job loss
4. Bankruptcy
5. Retirement
6. Deceased loved ones
7. Investor burnout

Figure 5.1

chasing distressed sellers' houses, you are relieving them of what may very well be a heavy burden and thereby freeing them to focus on the immediate needs that are more important to them at that particular time in their lives.

Transfer or Relocation

When was the last time you moved into a house and thought to yourself that you would stay in that location for an indefinite period of time, perhaps as long as 10 or more years? If you're anything like me, it probably wasn't that long ago. Although I've lived in some houses that I knew were only temporary, I've also lived in others that I thought were more permanent. It seems, however, that just about the time our family finally gets all the pictures unpacked and hung on the wall, we start thinking about moving again for one reason or another. Studies show that families living in the United States tend to be fairly mobile, moving on average every three to five years. While the reasons for moving vary considerably, one of the most common reasons is a change in a person's employment. It's not at all uncommon, for instance, for an employer to transfer an employee to another location. The transfer doesn't have to be out of state to necessitate a move. For example, if the branch manager of a bank located on the south side of a large metropolitan area such as Atlanta was reassigned to manage a new branch opening up on the north side of town, the difference in driving one way could be as much as 30 minutes to an hour. If the branch manager lived on the south end of town, she would now have to commute an additional 30 minutes or more each way. Depending on where her spouse worked, there's a good chance the family would eventually move closer to the bank's new branch to reduce the amount of time spent on the road each day.

Although employees sometime know well in advance of an impending move and have ample time to sell their houses at full market price, other times they have very little notice and must price their houses to facilitate faster sales. While some larger employers provide financial assistance to employees who are being transferred, this tends to be more of the exception than the rule. Most employers give their employees a choice of absorbing the expense of moving on their own or simply being terminated. Those individuals not receiving the benefit of financial assistance may find themselves in the position of having to make two house payments. For example, if the first house hasn't sold before the new job starts in another area, the employee will be forced to find housing in the new area while simultaneously making payments on both houses. This situation can create a financial hardship, especially under prolonged circumstances. Sellers facing this type of situation are often highly motivated and thereby more flexible on the asking price of their houses. They may even be willing to provide buyers with some type of creative financing terms as well.

I found myself in that very position several years ago. My wife and I bought a new house in Michigan that we were required to close on, even though we had not yet sold our home in Texas. After about six months of making payments on both houses, a buyer offered me much less than what similar houses in the neighborhood were selling for. Although I was disappointed at having received a low offer, I was also grateful to be relieved of having to make the house payment on the unoccupied, non-income-producing house in Texas. The buyer, on the other hand, got a great deal, and I'm quite confident that he could sell it today for much more than he paid for it then.

One way to locate sellers who have been transferred is through a real estate agent. Sales agents can search the MLS using any number of search criteria. In this example, they might use terms such as *transfer* or *relocation*. Another term the agent can use to search with is *VLB*, which means "vacant on lock box." This is an indication that the seller has already moved into another house and is now most likely in the position of having to make dual house payments. Real estate agents can also search the additional notes or comments section for descriptive terms that may indicate the seller has been transferred. An example of one such phrase would be "Must sell! Seller transferred. Will consider all offers!" Another way to locate undervalued properties of this type is by searching the classified newspapers. Check the FSBO (for sale by owner) section as well as the classified ads placed by agents. With the exception of VLB, you'll want to look for terminology similar to that found in the MLS. Remember that the average family moves every three to five years and that many of them are relocating to another area. With the highly nomadic population we have in the United States, you're sure to find plenty of opportunities of this type.

Divorce

The word *divorce* describes the act or instance of separating one thing from another. The term is frequently used to refer to a married couple who have legally separated. By its very definition, when a couple divorces, they separate from each other. In other words, they go their separate ways. This means that at least one spouse in the relationship will move out of the house and oftentimes both spouses will move. Sadly enough, statistics show that nearly one out of two marriages ends in divorce. This all too common separation often creates a financial hardship for the family, especially if it is a more traditional household in which the father is the provider and the mother is a stay-at-home mom who functions as the primary caregiver for younger children. In a situation like this, all members of the family are affected, and where one larger house was adequate before, two smaller houses or apartments will be necessary now. Although some couples are able to separate under amicable conditions, more often than not there are feelings of hurt, anger, and resentment. In this type of environment, it is difficult for spouses to work together when deciding who gets what, especially where the house is concerned. In some instances, the house is sold without really caring about attaining full market price. For example, if one spouse has moved out of the house and is now renting an apartment but is also responsible for making the house payment, a financial hardship may have been created. As far as this spouse is concerned, the sooner the house can be sold, the better. Furthermore, when the house is finally sold, this spouse knows that whatever net proceeds remain will have to be split with the other spouse. In this embittered state of mind, one spouse may not want the other spouse to have anything, even if it means that neither will get anything. This seemingly irrational behavior is the result of years of love, compassion, and intimacy with each other that are now nothing more than a shattered dream. While love is a powerful emotion, hate can be equally powerful.

Locating houses that have been put on the market by divorcing couples is easier than you may think. When a couple files for divorce, they must file a document known as a divorce decree, which is a legally binding command or decision entered on the court record issued by a court or judge. Divorce decrees are recorded and become public documents that are usually considered part of court files. In most states, they are filed at the Superior Court clerk's office of the county in which the divorce was granted. Public records are exactly that—public. There are few, if any, restrictions on the release of public records, including divorce records. Information from public records, including divorce records, is frequently compiled by businesses and made available to those parties who may be interested in them. Public records may also be used by private investigators, attorneys, law enforcement officials, other government agencies, and by consumers like you. With more public records being stored in computer databases, information has become easier to retrieve than ever before. In many instances, public records can be obtained directly online and oftentimes free of charge. If you are interested in pursuing undervalued real estate opportunities that may be caused by divorce, I recommend contacting one of the clerks who works in the records department at your local county courthouse and asking for the name of a legal guide or publication that might contain the information. The clerk should be able to refer you to the best source for this type of information. After you have obtained a list of recently divorced couples, you can then mail literature to them about your company, stating that you are an investor who buys houses and that if they are interested in selling, you would like to have the opportunity to work with them to purchase their house. Explain in your letter that it is best if they contact you first, before listing the house with a real estate agent, so that they can save themselves the commission. This tactic can give you the advantage over other potential buyers by putting you at the head of the line. If you get to look at the house first and are able to negotiate a sale that is agreeable to both you and the sellers, then you will have eliminated your competitors with this one easy-to-use technique.

Job Loss

Another life-changing event that has a significant impact on families is directly related to changes in one or more of the spouses' financial condition. The most likely cause of financial hardship is a change in employment circumstances. Homeowners who may have been caught in the latest round of "downsizing" or "rightsizing"— or whatever the current buzz word may be—are very likely to be distressed, especially those who have only a minimum amount of cash reserves in savings. With changes in economic conditions occurring almost routinely, it is difficult to predict when the next Enron will go belly up and wreak havoc on the lives of thousands of employees, not to mention the tens of thousands of investors who have placed their faith and trust in companies such as this. I truly believe that the majority of executives running corporate America are good and honest people who have our best interests at heart. These types of leaders, however, seldom make the headlines. It's the Enrons and WorldComs that capture our attention and, unfortunately, the negative publicity tends to spill over to the other 99 percent of businesses that are providing jobs for us. The result is that many of these corporate leaders are demonized in the process and the prevailing attitude toward them becomes one of mistrust. In addition, the cyclical nature of business, which rises and falls with the ebb and flow of the economy, causes disruptions in the workforce. Just as an individual would not work for free (unless it were for a charitable cause), so are corporations in business to make a profit. If the marginal return on invested capital does not meet the investors' minimum standards, operations are typically altered or otherwise modified to improve returns. In some instances, these modifications may include paring down labor costs just to stay in business. While it is unfortunate that some employees lose their jobs, it is better than shutting down an entire company and causing a total and complete loss for all its employees.

For those employees who have been unfortunate enough to be caught in the crossfire of corporate layoffs, the results can sometimes be devastating. Unless there are substantial cash reserves readily available in a liquid form, such as a money market account, an immediate reduction in spending is almost always the outcome. This is followed by the sale of nonessential assets such as boats, motorcycles, and ski-mobiles. Newer vehicles are traded in for older ones, and eventually, if work is not found soon enough, the larger house is sold for a smaller and more affordable one. Your role as an investor is to locate sellers who have motivating reasons to sell their houses quickly and will offer a substantial amount of pricing concessions because of their misfortunes. While finding people who have recently lost their jobs may not be an exact science, there are certain steps that can be taken to identify those areas that are known to have been affected by a downturn in the economy. For instance, corporate layoffs, plant closings, and facility shutdowns are generally well publicized by local media outlets. By being aware of similar developments in your area, you can focus on those neighborhoods most likely to have been affected by layoffs. Oftentimes, certain communities are known to have a high percentage of people who were working at the same place of employment. When a manufacturing facility closes down, for example, there may be a higher than normal concentration of families in a given community who are adversely affected and consequently may have no choice but to sell their homes. You can make those residents aware of your services by placing signs throughout the neighborhood that say something like, "I buy houses. Fast closings. Call (800) 555-5555." Another effective way to contact them is to send direct mail pieces, such as postcards, to an entire neighborhood within a specific zip code, again advertising your services as a real estate investor. When dealing with people who have recently lost their jobs, remember to be sensitive to their plight by treating them with dignity and respect. You're not out to rake them over the coals and strip them of their pride, but rather to make the best deal that is mutually acceptable to both of you.

Bankruptcy

In the previous section, we discussed the devastating effects the loss of employment can have on individuals or families. Sometimes those effects are so far reaching as to force these people into personal bankruptcy. The loss of employment, however, is not the only cause of bankruptcy. As consumers take on ever-increasing amounts of debt, the ability to repay that debt becomes increasingly difficult. Encouraged by historically low interest rates and the mantra of "buy today and pay tomorrow," more and more consumers have discovered that they can no longer afford to keep up with the payments demanded by their creditors. By borrowing from one source to pay another, the cycle of debt becomes increasingly vicious, much like a malignant cancer accelerating out of control until it ultimately vanquishes its victim.

Just as certain documents pertaining to a divorce are made a matter of public record, so are documents pertaining to bankruptcy. Also, like divorce records, bankruptcy records are compiled by data vendors who resell the information to consumers. Bankruptcy notices or records can be found in legal publications that serve a particular county, as well as from online sources. One such source is a national company named InfoUSA (www.infousa.com), and to my knowledge, it is one of the largest, if not the largest, compiler of public records and consumer information in the United States. The company asserts:

Our file is the most comprehensive consumer database of U.S. households in the industry. We aggregate over 2 billion records annually from 4,300 telephone directories and 35 other proprietary sources. Our file includes the most recent transactions of households that have moved across the country, ensuring the most accurate and comprehensive data available in the industry. We are able to identify 300,000 household moves with telephone numbers and integrate them into the database monthly, as well as provide weekly updates with telephone numbers from a separate New Mover File. Our recent investment in data provides fresher, more complete and comprehensive name, address, and phone coverage.

With respect to the company's bankruptcy database, InfoUSA boasts that it "is a comprehensive, nationwide file which contains bankruptcy and tax lien information on over 30 million individuals and businesses," and that the "information is gathered from federal, state, and county courthouses and from other public record sources. Approximately 75,000 new records are added to the database each month." Leads from the bankruptcy database can be selected from any one of the following categories.

Bankruptcy type
Bankruptcy status
City
County
State
Zip code
Filing date

Purchasing leads from a national vendor like InfoUSA is the easiest and most efficient way I know of to quickly build a contact file for your own area. You can then mail your marketing literature that offers your services as an investor. One caveat to be aware of when dealing with individuals who have filed for bankruptcy is that there's a good chance many of their assets may be frozen. In other words, in some cases, they won't be able to sell to you even if they want to because the court must follow a specific process.

Retirement

Retirement is yet another circumstance that has a significant effect on a family's income. At some time in everyone's life, they reach a point at which they are ready to retire. With the aging baby boomer population, there are more people than ever who are retiring. Although we tend to think of those who are preparing for retirement as financially sound and getting ready to live a life of luxury and enjoyment, this is not always the case. Studies show Americans save less money on average than people of other industrialized nations. Average Americans save only 4 percent of their income, and many do not even save that. In our fast paced and sometimes impatient society of "buy it today and pay for it tomorrow," many people have become so accustomed to living from paycheck to paycheck that they can scarcely afford to retire. Some of these older citizens who are approaching the age of retirement, however, do not even realize that they cannot retire and maintain the same standard of living they've always enjoyed. They mistakenly believe that the Social Security benefits received from Uncle Sam along with what little they have in savings will be sufficient to sustain them upon retirement. After a few short months of living the so-called good life, they discover all too late that their financial resources are limited. By then, however, it's usually too late because they have already retired and pride or circumstances prevent them from going back to work. For those retirees lucky enough to own their homes free and clear, selling the homes represents a viable opportunity to free up some much needed cash. The logical step for many such individuals is to sell their houses and move into smaller and more affordable homes. This process enables them to free up a substantial portion of their life savings, which had accumulated over many years, while simultaneously reducing their insurance payments and property tax liability.

In addition to changes in financial conditions for senior citizens, changes in health can also affect housing choices. The correlation between increases in age and deteriorating health conditions are well documented. Poor health often creates special needs, such as a need for assisted living, and thereby contributes to the need for a change in housing. As the owner of several model homes in our new home communities, my sales agents have shared with me all too often the plight of senior citizens who have these concerns. I can't think of a single instance when an elderly couple has come to us looking to purchase a larger home than the one they already have. The two most common requests are a smaller, more affordable home and a single-level, or one-story, home. They want to reduce their monthly obligations, and they don't want to climb stairs anymore. The reasons for these two conditions may vary somewhat, but they are typically related to a reduction in the couple's financial resources and declining health conditions. It is certainly not my intent to imply in this section that all senior citizens are doomed to a life of financial and physical hardship, but rather to suggest that the propensity for these situations to occur is much more likely for senior citizens than it is for younger citizens.

Several years ago, I purchased a 25-unit apartment building from an older couple who had reached retirement age. It just so happened that the couple had owned the apartment complex for exactly 25 years and had just made their very last mortgage payment. Selling the apartments would provide them with a considerable lump sum of cash that would allow them to retire under more comfortable circumstances. Although they could have continued to live off the rental income generated by the building, cashing out would enable them to leave the apartment business altogether and thereby provide them with both time and money, two commodities that we rarely possess at the same time. As the saying goes, people tend to have either more time than money or more money than time, but rarely do they have both at the same time. Although this couple was an elderly couple, I wouldn't necessarily consider them to be distressed sellers. I think in this case the term *motivated sellers* would be more appropriate. The couple could easily have continued on just as they had for the previous 25 years; however, because they had reached the age of retirement, they were anxious to make a change. We ended up negotiating the transaction in such a manner as to give them a price slightly below market and most of their money in cash at closing through third-party financing. In return, they gave me great terms on the deal by their willingness to take back a second mortgage for the remaining balance. I also received a large credit at closing to be used for miscellaneous repairs and improvements, which further reduced the amount of cash I needed to purchase the apartments.

By now, I think you will agree with me that there are opportunities to find undervalued properties that fall into this segment. You may be thinking, however, that while all of this sounds good on the surface, how in the world do you go about finding retirees who are trying to sell their houses? They certainly don't put a sign in the yard that says "Retiring. Must Sell!" There is also typically no indication given in a classified ad or even in the MLS. Okay, so if you can't find any information through these more traditional methods, how exactly do you go about finding this type of information? To find undervalued properties that fall into this group, demographic data is the key. There are numerous national services that provide all kinds of information about consumers. In fact, sometimes the amount and type of data that has been collected on us is downright scary. Information about one's age, household income, and consumer preferences is readily available through these sources. Referring once again to InfoUSA, the following categories represent a few of the many types of information that is readily available to consumers.

New homeowners
New movers

Millionaires and multimillionaires
Newborns and prenatal information
Boat owners
Pilots
Insurance agents
Ailments of various people
Occupations
Occupant addresses
Real estate agents and brokers
Teachers at school
Teachers at home
Nurses
High school students
College students
Military veterans
Motorcycle owners
Bankruptcy declarers
All types of magazine subscribers

Name, age, and address information for retirees or senior citizens also is readily available and can be purchased in a label format or in a database file format. I suggest purchasing the information on disk in a file format so that it can be used more than once. Once you've built a small database of individuals who fall into this group, you can send a flyer or other type of direct mail piece to them to advertise your services. The idea is to keep your name in front of them on a recurring basis, perhaps as often as once each quarter. Let them know that you are in the business of buying houses and that should the need arise, you will be happy to discuss with them the services that you offer. Remember that you are not out to take unfair advantage of this group of sellers, or any other sellers for that matter. You are, however, in business to purchase undervalued properties and if the seller's needs and your needs match, then everybody comes out a winner!

Estate Sales

The term *estate sale* is used to describe the process of selling both real and personal property upon the death of its owner. For example, when an elderly person dies, a family member such as a son or daughter is often left with the responsibility of settling the estate. That individual is typically referred to as the *executor* of the estate. After the family has removed personal objects of sentimental value, they often choose to dispose of any remaining items by contacting an experienced estate seller. While it may seem somewhat morbid and disrespectful to the deceased to rummage through their homes and personal property after they have died, estate sales actually serve a useful purpose in that they make an already difficult time for the surviving family a little bit easier by simplifying the process of disposing of their loved one's assets. Estate sales are especially helpful for adult children who may have to sell a house and clear out the contents after a parent's death. In many such instances, the house is offered for sale along with all of the personal property. Sometimes the family members of the deceased will offer the estate sale themselves in order to avoid having to give a percentage of the sales away. As a general rule, however, the better estate sales are those that are organized by professional estate sale companies which will typically agree to take on an estate sale only if they believe the items that are available for sale are plentiful enough and of high enough quality to be worth their while.

Although you may be able to find some unique and interesting items in an estate sale, what you're really after is the house. To find houses that may be offered in an estate sale, you can simply contact the estate sale companies in your area. Explain to them that you are an investor interested in buying bargain-priced property and ask them to notify you when they hold estate sales that offer houses that meet your investment criteria. Estate sale listings also can be found in the classified section of most newspapers under the heading of "Estate Sales." Another place to search for undervalued properties that fall into this category is the obituaries section of the newspaper. In fact, because this information is readily available online, you can search multiple newspapers in your area with the click of a mouse. Although an obituary provides information about a deceased individual, it generally provides information about surviving family members as well. This is important to you because it is the surviving family members who will need to be contacted about selling the house. You can collect the names and addresses of the surviving members and put them in your database of other potential undervalued property contacts and mail them a flyer or brochure about the services you provide.

Single-family houses offered for sale on behalf of a deceased family member such as a parent can oftentimes be purchased below market value because the family members faced with liquidating the assets do not necessarily want to hold out for top dollar. Their objective is to get the house sold as quickly as possible, pay off the note if there is one, and split the proceeds among the siblings. If the parent is an elderly person, there's a good chance they have lived in their house for 20 or 30 years and that they owned it free and clear at the time of their passing. This represents a golden opportunity for the children who are left behind since they now are the beneficiaries of the property. Although they would like to get the best price possible for the house, if a creative investor such as yourself offers to cash them out in 30 days provided they can offer the house to you at the right price (one that is below market), there's a good chance they will jump at your offer. This is especially true if there is very little or no debt remaining on the house. While being respectful of their deceased parent, the children are quite likely to already be envisioning how they will use their share of the proceeds once the sale is completed. This is a natural process and is not meant to reflect negatively on family members who have lost a loved one. Like most of us, the family members are likely to have financial obligations such as an auto loan or credit card debt that they are thinking about paying off. So while holding out for the absolute best price on their parents' house would be the ideal situation, selling for all cash in 30 days at a discount to market will sound pretty good to them too.

Investor Burnout

Investor burnout is another primary reason for people to sell their houses. They excitedly purchase their first few rental houses with the notion that at last they have made it. Then reality sets in. The tenants call complaining about the broken air conditioner, or the dishwasher that needs replacing. Then there's Uncle Joe who just died and they have to help Aunt Sally with the funeral expenses, so they don't have this month's rent. I've heard enough excuses in my experience to fill a book. I remember one lady who did everything she could to avoid paying her rent. On one occasion, she stopped by our office to pay her rent. She was in a hurry as she was on her way to work. In the blink of an eye, the lady dropped off a check and was out the door. "Thank you," I called out to her as she whisked away. The amount of rent due from the lady was $575. I vividly remember glancing down at the check and then feeling my blood boil as I realized the amount of the check she wrote was $5.75, not $575! Since I knew she worked right down the street, I quickly hopped in my car and confronted her about the error. She acted surprised about the slight oversight, as if she didn't know, but I think she was more surprised by the fact that I caught up with her than anything else. She wrote another check on the spot, and this time it was for the correct amount. Stories like this can be enough to discourage even the best of investors who are managing their own properties.

Another reason that investors suffer from burnout is because they are unprepared for what all property ownership entails. For example, if an inexperienced investor who just purchased her first rental property paid full price for a house that she put nothing down on, then she has quite possibly created a situation in which the maximum use of leverage has caused the property to have a negative cash flow. In other words, by the time she pays the principal, interest, taxes, insurance, maintenance, and repairs on the house, not only is there nothing left, but she must actually come up with money each month just to break even. Without the proper resources such as a savings account with several months of reserves in it, she may soon discover that she can no longer afford to keep up with the negative cash flow. This is particularly true the first time a major repair is required, such as replacing a furnace or an air-conditioning unit. A major expenditure may then cause her to fall behind with her monthly obligation to the lender. With no reserves and a negative cash flow, the inexperienced investor may be forced to jump ship and will most likely be happy if she can just get out from under the payment and the stress of managing the property. Investor burnout has quickly turned her into a "don't wanter," as in, "I don't wanter no more!" If conditions of distress persist, these investors sometimes feel like they are pushed to the point of no return, and when that happens, they become burned out and throw in the towel. They've been beaten up enough and are ready to be out of the real estate business. In some cases, they can't get rid of what has now become nothing more than a headache soon enough. The prospect of making any money on the deal is long gone. Aspirations of success have instead turned to a longing for survival. If their circumstances are really desperate, they just want to stop the bleeding.

In the case of investor burnout, the degree of the seller's motivation will correlate directly with his degree of distress. This is where subtle clues can be detected by direct communication with the seller. For example, he may make sarcastic remarks about the tenant being late with her payments all the time, or that he's tired of being a landlord. The seller may also be much more direct and tell you in no uncertain terms that he can't keep up with the payments and that he doesn't want the headache of managing property anymore. If the seller is suffering from burnout related to managing his property, he will most likely be highly motivated, and a highly motivated seller is a flexible seller. It is situations like this that you want to be on the lookout for.

Investor-type don't wanter properties may be advertised in the classified section of the newspaper or be listed in the MLS as a rental or
investment property, or the owner may even respond to one of your
many signs that are strategically placed to advertise that you buy
houses. The dialogue you conduct with the seller will reveal his true
motive for disposing of the property. You can start with a simple question like, "Why are you selling?" Give them time to respond and then
follow up with more specific questions. The seller may tell you, for
example, that she is getting a new job and no longer has time to manage her property. You may respond by congratulating her on the new
job and then asking a follow-up question like, "How long has your
rental house been vacant?" If it's obvious that the house has been
empty for several months, you know immediately that there is no cash
flowing in. Another follow-up question might be, "Are the payments
current on the house?" If she responds that yes, they are current, but
that she is having a hard time keeping up with them, then there's a
good possibility that she is a highly motivated seller and will therefore
be willing to negotiate on price with you. There are plenty of sellers in
situations similar to this. The more involved you become in real estate
and the more contacts you develop, the more you will come across
opportunities such as this.

In summary, there are many events that occur in the lives of people
that may cause abnormal or undue distress, which in turn can create
opportunities to purchase property at bargain prices. In this chapter,
we discussed the impact of several of these life-changing events on
individuals. They include job transfers, divorce, the loss of employment by one or both spouses, filing for personal bankruptcy, reaching
the golden years and settling into a life of retirement, estate sales, and,
finally, investor burnout. By working with distressed sellers who are
undergoing personal difficulties, you are actually helping them by
relieving them of what can be a tremendous source of stress. Sellers
experiencing life-changing events such as the ones described in this

chapter are all too glad to be relieved of their mortgages. Selling their houses is secondary to a more immediate and fundamental need that has arisen due to what are often unforeseen circumstances. By purchasing distressed sellers' houses, you are relieving them of what may very well be a heavy burden and thereby freeing them to focus on more immediate needs that are more important to them at that particular time in their lives.

6

How You Can Help Distressed Lenders by Purchasing Their Undervalued Properties

In Chapter 4, we focused on locating undervalued *properties* that are said to be in distress and may be available for sale. In Chapter 5, we learned about locating *sellers* who are said to be in distress and may have undervalued properties for sale. In this chapter, we will study third parties who are said to be in distress. These third parties are most often *lenders* who have a financial interest in a property. Lenders become distressed when a borrower fails to meet certain contractual obligations set forth within legally binding agreements. A borrower is said to be in *default* when the repayment terms as stipulated in a contract such as a promissory note are not met. This is typically the result of a borrower's failing to make the payments as required in the contract. The term *foreclosure* is used to denote the process whereby legal action is taken by a lien holder such as a lender to repossess property held by a borrower who is in default. Lenders are said to be in distress because they are in the business of making loans and not in the business of repossessing the collateral or security attached to those loans. When a borrower defaults, the loan becomes a nonperforming asset, at which time it is no longer earning interest. If a loan is not earning interest, it is not producing income for the lender. These nonperforming loans actually cost the lender more money because of the lost earning power of the assets deployed, as well as any legal and administrative costs that may be associated with collecting the loan. Lenders who hold nonperforming assets such as real estate owned, or REOs, are highly motivated sellers, and therein lies the opportunity for astute investors to discover the many advantages available in this market.

Although buying foreclosed properties has frequently been left to professional real estate investors, the record number of foreclosures in recent years has made it easier than ever for even beginning investors to purchase them. The key to successfully purchasing undervalued properties in this market is to develop a comprehensive understanding of the foreclosure process by familiarizing yourself with each of its four phases (see Figure 6.1). The first of these four phases is referred to as the *preforeclosure phase* and involves negotiating with homeowners and gaining control of their property. The second phase is the *sheriff's sale* at which time property is sold at a public auction. The third phase of the foreclosure process occurs during a period of time referred to as the *redemption period*. The redemption period is a period of time established by law in most states, but not all, whereby the homeowner has the right to *redeem* himself or herself by bringing current all obligations that brought about the foreclosure process to begin with. The fourth phase of the foreclosure process is referred to as the *postforeclosure phase*. In this phase, ownership rights of the property now belong to the

Four Phases of the Foreclosure Process

1. Preforeclosure opportunities
2. Foreclosure and sheriff's sales
3. Redemption period
4. Postforeclosure market and lender REOs

Figure 6.1

lending institution that brought about the foreclosure action. Opportunities to purchase property exist in each of these four phases. Investors should be aware of the advantages, as well as the disadvantages, of buying in each.

Preforeclosure Opportunities

The first phase of the foreclosure process is referred to as the *preforeclosure phase* since the actual foreclosure action has not yet occurred. In this phase, the borrower has missed at least one payment and is now considered to be delinquent on the loan. The problem is exacerbated with each passing month as the borrower continues to fall behind on the required payments. The more time that passes, the greater the problem becomes until, eventually, the lender is left with no choice but to take legal action. Recall that the lender is not in the real estate business and much prefers the borrower to bring the loan current. Meanwhile, the further behind the borrower gets in payments, the more difficult it becomes to bring the loan current. It also is quite probable that by this time the borrower has defaulted on other obligations as well. Smaller consumer loans such as credit cards are usually the first debts that are not paid, followed by auto loans and home equity loans. Most homeowners will make every effort to hang on to their houses for as long as possible, until finally there just isn't any money left to make the payments. When individuals default on their home loans, it's a pretty good indication that they have exhausted all other resources. Therein lies the problem—as well as the opportunity. The lender wants nothing more than to get paid, while the homeowner would like nothing more than to pay the lender. As a third-party investor, you have the opportunity to bring value to this conundrum by negotiating on behalf of the homeowners. Although you are not there to bail them out of a situation they got themselves into, you can at least offer the homeowners a way out that will minimize the damage to their credit and, perhaps more importantly, to their self-worth and dignity. By negotiating with the lender on their behalf, you can agree to bring the payments current, offer the homeowners a small amount of cash to help them move, and either take over the loan using a *subject to agreement* or refinance the current loan with the same lender or another lender of your choice.

One primary advantage of purchasing homes in the preforeclosure market is the ability to minimize your risk exposure and initial cash outlay to gain control of a property. The subject to agreement allows you to gain control of the property by having the homeowner quitclaim the deed to you, thereby giving you legal control of it. The lender will most likely not foreclose on the property so long as the payments are being made, which is now, of course, your responsibility. A subject to agreement is an effective way of gaining control of the property without assuming any liability for it since the loan is still in the original homeowner's name. Although the legal ownership of the property has been transferred to you as the investor, the seller is still liable for the underlying promissory note. Because the note has not been fully satisfied, the lender still holds the mortgage, which provides the lender with a legal interest in the property. If, for whatever reason, you did not make the monthly payments, it is the seller whom the lender will foreclose on and not you. Your intent, however, is to assume control of the property, find another buyer for it, and make a profit. Anything less than that would represent a waste of your time and resources. The subject to agreement minimizes an investor's risk exposure while attempting to find another buyer for the property. When a new buyer is found, he or she will be responsible for obtaining a new loan on the property in order to pay off the existing loan that is still in the name of the original homeowner.

One of the main disadvantages to buying real estate in the preforeclosure stage is the difficulty of getting homeowners to allow you to intervene on their behalf. First of all, you have to get their attention by getting them to respond to you. Homeowners in this stage of the process are likely to have been contacted by numerous other investors either through direct mail, by telephone, or in person, as well as by numerous mortgage brokers seeking to refinance their loan. Although it may seem that no lender would be interested in refinancing a loan for sellers who cannot make the payments on their current loan, this is not the case. There are many lenders who specialize in this type of market and who are quite willing to lend money provided that the loan-to-value ratio is low enough and there is enough equity in the property. For example, if the loan-to-value ratio were only 50 percent and a lender lent $100,000 on a $200,000 house, the lender's position is actually quite secure. If the homeowner now defaults on the new loan, the new lender can comfortably foreclose on the property, recoup the original amount of the loan, and quite possibly sell the house at a profit. Once again, as an investor, you are competing against a myriad of other investors as well as lenders like the one described in this example. Under these circumstances, it can be difficult to gain the confidence and trust of homeowners who can no longer make their payments.

There are several ways to locate undervalued properties that fall into the preforeclosure category. These methods depend on whether or not a state is a *title theory* state or a *lien theory* state. In title theory states that use a trust deed, formal notice that a borrower is in default is given by the filing of a *notice of default* in the county in which the property exists. In lien theory states that use a mortgage, a *lis pendens* is filed. Regardless of which instrument is filed, both serve the same purpose, which is to make an official communication and a public notice that one party intends to bring about some type of legal action against another party. Since these notices are a matter of public record filed at the appropriate county courthouse, they are easily ascertained and signal the beginning of the foreclosure process. To obtain a copy of these records, you can do the research at the courthouse yourself, subscribe to a newspaper that publishes legal notices, or subscribe to an online service specializing in providing this type of information. Unless you have the time to spend at the county courthouse researching public records, I recommend subscribing to a service that will provide this information to you, preferably in an electronic format that allows you to sort and search easily by criteria specified by you. Whatever methods you decide to use, keep in mind that because there are other investors using the same methods to contact homeowners in the preforeclosure phase, you will have to figure out a way to differentiate yourself from them. Both frequency of contact and persistence are the keys to success in the preforeclosure market.

Foreclosure and Sheriff's Sales

The second phase of the foreclosure process occurs at the *sheriff's sale* and denotes the period of time when the default or preforeclosure phase of the property has expired. It is in this phase that the property is auctioned off at the county courthouse in a public sale to the highest bidder, which is usually the lender. With the exception of the redemption period, the sale terminates the rights bestowed by the homeowner's interest in the property. The proceeds from the sale are disbursed to the lender bringing the foreclosure action first, which is most often the lender holding the first mortgage. If the proceeds are adequate to satisfy the first lien holder's position, additional funds are then used to settle any remaining obligations in the order they were recorded. Remaining funds, if any, are disbursed to the homeowner. In some states, if the debt to the lender was not fully satisfied, the lender can file an additional lawsuit with the courts to obtain a *deficiency judgment*. A deficiency judgment is issued to recover the difference between the full amount that was owed to the lender and the amount that was actually collected at the auction.

The chief advantage of purchasing property at the auction is the ability to buy houses at bargain-basement prices with minimal competition. Oftentimes the only other party you may be bidding against is a representative from the lending institution. Since the lenders have no desire to take back the property, they actually *want* you to outbid the company they are representing. Lenders have a predetermined minimum threshold that must be met, so don't assume that it is possible to bid a ridiculously low amount, such as one dollar. As in most investment opportunities, there is a positive correlation between risk and reward— the higher the risk, the higher the potential reward. The potential rewards of buying at an auction are high because the properties for sale can be purchased at a discount with a minimal amount of competition.

The primary disadvantage of purchasing property at an auction is the increased risk exposure resulting from any liens that may have been filed against the property. Although an abstract showing the history of a property may have been pulled, it is not always possible to know or be aware of every encumbrance that may be attached to it. Before actually bidding on property at an auction, a title search should be done as early as possible so as to have ample time to research its chain of title. On the day prior to the auction sale, the title search should be updated in case any last-minute liens were filed by other parties who may have had a claim against the property since this represents the last opportunity to recoup any losses incurred by them. The last thing you want to do is find yourself stuck with a property that has additional liens attached to it that you were unaware of at the time of the auction. Another disadvantage of purchasing at an auction stems from the amount of cash required to participate in this type of transaction. At the time of the bidding, a 5 to 10 percent deposit is typically required in the form of a cashier's check. The funds for the balance of the purchase price are usually due within a few days and sometimes even the same day as the auction. For many investors, raising that much cash in such a short time is very difficult. That's one reason why the competition at auction sales is often limited to just a handful of buyers, and sometimes not even that many. It helps to have access to cash that can be raised immediately, perhaps from a large line of credit or from another investor. A third disadvantage of purchasing real estate at auction sales is the redemption period required in some states that gives owners of foreclosed property the right to "redeem" themselves by reclaiming the property. Finally, property scheduled for sale at an auction is sometimes canceled days before the sale because of the defaulting borrower's bringing the loan current at the last minute. This can be especially frustrating if you have gone through the trouble of researching the title and analyzing the property only to have the sale canceled at the last moment.

There are several ways to locate undervalued properties that fall into the sheriff's sale phase. The most obvious source for these properties is at the county courthouse where the sale will occur. A "notice of sale" is posted to announce publicly that the property in question will be sold to the highest bidder on a specific date and at a specific time and place. Notices are also often required to be published several weeks in advance in the newspapers that serve the area in which the property is located. In addition, many areas have legal newspapers you can subscribe to that have all of the legal notices published in them for a given area. They contain notices such as notices of default, notices of sale, marriage and divorce notices, building permit data, and much more. Finally, notice of sale data can also be found in an electronic format through a subscription service in some areas.

Redemption Period

The third phase of the foreclosure process is referred to as the *redemption period*. It is in this phase that the ownership rights of the property have been transferred to the successful bidder at the auction sale. In most instances, this is the bank or mortgage company that brought about the foreclosure action. Although the lending institution now technically owns the property, it may be limited by a state-mandated redemption period that gives the defaulting borrowers the opportunity to *redeem* themselves. In other words, if the borrower can come up with the full amount of money owed to the lenders, he or she has the legal right to redeem the property by purchasing it back from them. The defaulting parties rarely, however, come up with the funds required to purchase the property back. After all, if they had the money to buy the house, they wouldn't have defaulted to begin with. Whether or not your state has a redemption period will depend on whether or not it is a *title theory* or *lien theory* state. While most title theory states do not have mandatory redemption periods, most all lien theory states do. The redemption period can range anywhere from a few days to a few months and even as long as one year. During the redemption period, the new owner is precluded from selling the property until the period expires. Oftentimes the house is still occupied by the defaulting borrower who essentially gets to live in the house for free. As previously mentioned, this can be up to a full year in some states. That's a pretty good deal for the person or persons living there. Free rent for a year? Hmmm . . . Where do I sign?

By now you may be wondering how to purchase the property during this phase. If the lender purchased the property at an auction and the defaulting borrower has a period of time stipulated by the state to redeem it, how can an investor possibly buy the property? The answer lies in the defaulting borrower's *redemption rights*. Just as an option gives an investor the right to purchase property at a predetermined price, the redemption period gives the borrower the right to buy back his or her property at a predetermined price. And just as the rights granted in an option agreement can be sold or assigned, the rights granted in a redemption period can be sold or assigned. In other words, the default-ing borrower can sell or assign his or her redemption rights to an investor like yourself. If the defaulting borrower is still living in the house, you can offer $2,500, for example, to vacate the property and assign the right to redeem the property to you. This is very similar to purchasing an option on a property. An option grants a buyer the right to purchase property for a predetermined amount and for a specific period of time. If the buyer does not exercise the right to purchase within the stipulated period of time, the option expires worthless. Redemption rights grant the same rights to the party who holds them. If the rights are not exercised within the stated period of time, like the option, they expire worthless. Be aware that in some states redemption rights are not assignable. You may be able to circumvent this, however, by bringing the loan current for the borrower and having an agreement in place whereby he or she immediately quitclaims the deed to you upon doing so.

The main advantage of purchasing real estate during the redemption period is that many investors are not aware that redemption rights can be purchased during this period. They are instead waiting for the redemption period to expire so they can purchase the property from the lender after it does. This means less competition for you since there aren't many others going after foreclosed properties during this phase. Purchasing the redemption rights also gives you time to come up with financing for the property—that is, if you decide to purchase it. You may instead want to find another buyer for it. This enables you to transfer the property from the lender to the new buyer without having to take out a loan for it yourself. This strategy works especially well in states having long redemption periods such as six months or one year.

There are several ways to identify and locate properties that are in the redemption period. Recall the legal instruments that are filed in the county courthouse in the preforeclosure phase, which are referred to as the notice of default or the lis pendens. Depending on the state the property is located in, one of these two instruments is filed to give notice to the public that a suit is pending and that legal action is being brought against the defaulting borrower. A hearing is scheduled for the impending suit and, unless the matter is resolved, public notice is given once again and the property is eventually sold to the highest bidder at the auction sale. In each of these phases, the public is always kept apprised of the property's status through various public declarations. When a property is sold to the highest bidder at an auction sale, it becomes a matter of public record. In states having a redemption period, the clock starts ticking the day the property is sold. So, for example, in a state that has a six-month right of redemption period, an investor would have a full six months from the date of the auction sale to either procure another buyer for it or obtain financing sufficient to clear the debt owed to the lender. Because the sale of property at an auction is recorded and made a matter of public record, the information can be obtained by anyone. To obtain a copy of these records, you can do the research at the courthouse yourself, subscribe to a newspaper that publishes legal notices, or subscribe to an online service specializing in providing this type of information. If you don't have the time to spend at the county courthouse researching public records, I suggest that you subscribe to a service that will provide this information for you. The more rapidly you can act on the data provided, the more time you will have either to find another buyer or to obtain financing for it. This is especially important in states that have shorter redemption periods.

Postforeclosure Market and Lender REOs

The fourth phase of the foreclosure process is referred to as the *postforeclosure phase*. It is in this phase that the ownership rights of the property are now transferred to the lending institution that brought about the foreclosure action. The redemption period is past and the previous homeowner no longer enjoys any rights or claims to the property. When ownership is transferred to the lender's portfolio, it becomes a nonperforming asset and is referred to as *real estate owned*, or REO. Lenders are, of course, not in the business of managing real estate, nor do they want to be. The very nature of their business, however, demands that they assume risk with each and every loan extended to borrowers.

Unfortunately for the lenders, sometimes those borrowers default, and when they do, they have no choice but to foreclose on the property. The average lending institution's customers don't even know what a REO is or that they even exist. Lenders certainly don't promote the fact that they have real estate that has been foreclosed on and is now listed on their books as a nonperforming loan. Although almost all lenders have REOs, very few, if any, will publicize this information. That's not to say the information isn't available, but rather to say that lenders aren't in the habit of broadcasting this information to their general client base.

Two primary advantages of purchasing real estate in the postforeclosure market are the level of risk assumed and the availability of properties for sale. Unlike the auction market where there is potentially a high degree of uncertainty as to the chain of title and any encumbrances that may exist on a given piece of property, title issues in the postforeclosure market have generally been resolved. In other words, before the lender makes these properties available for sale, any liens or claims against the property other than that which the lender now has have all been resolved. The second primary benefit to purchasing real estate in this category is the availability of REOs that exist. In many areas, there exists an abundance of properties—quite often more than any single investor can manage individually. I don't mean to imply that REOs will fall into your lap with no effort on your part since that is certainly not the case. Time and energy are required to sift through the properties that are available to identify those opportunities that conform to your investment criteria. The fact that there are often many properties to choose from in this group that are free and clear of encumbrances leads to the biggest disadvantage of buying postforeclosure properties. The availability of properties and the ease of buying them quite naturally attract a greater number of buyers and thereby create more competition for them.

Lenders are usually somewhat flexible in their terms and conditions for selling a foreclosed property. Remember, they are in the business of lending money and not in the business of owning or managing real estate. The basis for the lender's initial asking price will likely be determined by the hard costs the bank has into it, or its book value. While the bank will no doubt make every effort to minimize its losses, if it is anxious to get the property off its books, there's a good chance it will be willing to negotiate with you by agreeing to write down a portion of the loan. Before making any offers to a lender, however, you should take time to physically inspect the property; determine the costs required for repairs, carrying costs, and transactions costs; and then make an offer based on your analysis. In other words, determine the maximum amount you can have into the deal and still make money on it based on a rate of return that is acceptable to you. If it doesn't make sense for you as an investor, you're better off letting the lender keep it. To avoid overpaying for a property, the bottom line is not to make the mistake of falling in love with it.

There are several ways to locate undervalued properties that fall into the postforeclosure category. The most obvious source for these properties is the lenders themselves. Smaller local lenders such as banks usually have one individual who is responsible for the real estate owned portfolio, while larger regional banks may have several people or even a department that is responsible for its nonperforming assets. Lenders dispose of these properties through a network of private investors who have expressed an interest in them, as well as through real estate agents who specialize in foreclosures. The network of private investors can include anyone. If you are interested in acquiring properties in this manner, then you will need to be prepared to do some initial legwork to establish the proper contacts. There is no limit to the number of lenders you can contact. I recommend establishing relationships with at least 8 to 10 lenders in your area to provide as large of a pool of foreclosed properties for sale as possible. Another very effective method of locating postforeclosure properties is through the network of real estate agents the lenders use to dispose of their properties. Agents specializing in this area often represent several lenders and typically have several REOs available for sale at any given time. You can find these agents by looking in the real estate publications that are distributed free of charge in various places such as grocery stores or office buildings. You can also call around to several local real estate offices and inquire as to who in their office specializes in foreclosures. Finally, another method of locating postforeclosure properties is through online services that specialize in providing this type of data. Most services are relatively inexpensive and require users to subscribe on a weekly or monthly basis. One primary drawback to using online services, however, is that the data provided by them is not always accurate. For example, in many instances, the data is not current. This can result in an inefficient use of the user's time and resources.

In summary, investors can purchase undervalued properties from distressed lenders in any one of four different phases, with each phase having its advantages and disadvantages. While gaining control of property in the preforeclosure phase can be accomplished with relatively very little capital, winning the confidence of the homeowner and competing against other investors can present a challenge. Purchasing property at an auction sale can be equally challenging since the condition of the title is not always known. The increase in risk, however, can potentially be offset by an increase in the return. In the third phase of the foreclosure process, investors may be able to gain control of a property by purchasing the redemption rights of the defaulting borrower. Not every state has redemption rights, however, and of those that do, some will not allow the borrower to assign his or her rights to another party. Finally, in the postforeclosure phase, undervalued REOs are readily available and provide lower-risk purchase opportunities than in other foreclosure phases. The low-risk opportunities available in this phase, however, attract more buyers and therefore bring a higher level of competitiveness for these properties. Regardless of which of these four phases an investor chooses to participate in, the ability to earn high-yielding profits can be realized by those who are patient, persistent, and prudent in their investment approach.

7

Undervalued Opportunities in New Construction

One source of finding potentially undervalued properties that is often overlooked by investors is newly constructed homes. As a builder myself, I am very familiar with the types of opportunities that become available throughout the residential construction industry. Opportunities arise from a variety of situations that occur on a routine basis. Some of these include developers, builders, and even home buyers who become distressed for one reason or another. Other reasons include the grand opening of a new community, the buildup of excess inventory, the final closeout of a community, and those regions that are experiencing rapid growth (see Figure 7.1).

```
        Undervalued Opportunities
           in New Construction

   1. Distressed developers
   2. Distressed builders
   3. Distressed home buyers
   4. Introductory sales
   5. Excess inventory
   6. Final closeout sales
   7. High-growth markets
```

Figure 7.1

Distressed Developers

A real estate developer's role is to take a piece of raw, undeveloped land, find a use for it, and convert it into land that is suitable for the purpose intended by the developer. This process necessitates determining the land's highest and best use, which is most often determined by market supply and demand functions. The developer may decide that a particular parcel of land is best used as a national championship golf course, or perhaps a commercial strip center, or maybe a residential community. Land used for developmental purposes often lies on the fringes or outlying areas of growing communities. The growth may be concentric, which means that land is developed outward from a centralized area in fairly equal amounts. The effect is similar to that of throwing a pebble into a pond, which in turn creates outward ripples from the point at which the pebble enters the water. All real estate development growth patterns are not necessarily concentric, however, as growth often occurs around traffic patterns that flow to and from major employment centers, as well as around areas that provide easy access to interstate freeways and highways.

Since it is the developer's responsibility to ascertain the feasibility of a project, he or she bears the risk of recognizing market demands and responding accordingly. If the developer's assessment is incorrect, thousands of dollars may already have been invested that will be difficult, at best, to recoup. Before developers can bring the projects to their completed states, however, they must first work together in a cooperative effort with other professionals, including engineers, surveyors, attorneys, architects, and various governmental bodies. Before the final approvals are granted, *if* they are granted, a number of challenges must be overcome. Some of these include water runoff and retention, density requirements, environmental issues, possible zoning changes, and appeasing local governmental agencies that often take it upon themselves to exercise more authority than they legally have. For example, members of a planning commission have an obligation to review projects in a timely manner to ensure they conform to zoning laws and local ordinances. It has been my experience that planning commission members often impose their own subjective opinions into the design and development of a project. If a change in zoning or a variance is being requested, they have every right to offer their opinions. If, however, a project is submitted that already fully complies with existing zoning requirements and local ordinances, their duty lies in reviewing and then approving the project and nothing more. All too often, however, members of the various agencies and boards responsible for approving projects become intoxicated with their own power and take it upon themselves to abuse the limitations of their authority by requiring developers to conform to standards that don't legally exist. Developers have the right, of course, to challenge these agencies in the courts, but doing so will mean costly delays. However, once a developer's project receives its final approval and all applicable permits, the developer is then ready to prepare the site for its intended use. Preparation of a site includes activities such as grading, excavating, laying underground utilities, installing storm water systems, and building roads. Depending on the size of the project, the developer is likely to have committed several hundred thousand dollars by this time.

After obtaining all the necessary approvals and completing the development and construction of a parcel, a developer is then ready to begin selling lots. Developers typically attempt to presell as many lots as they can in order to pay down the debt incurred throughout the different phases of the project. If possible, they may work with builders who will purchase either all of the lots or a significant portion of them. Sometimes they are successful in their efforts to presell lots and sometimes they are not. If sales are slow, developers may not be able to meet their financial obligations to the lenders to pay down the debt that is carried on the land. This type of situation can easily cause a developer to become distressed. With each month that passes with no sale of lots, a developer will become increasingly anxious to dispose of what are now becoming unwanted lots. Forget about the prospect of making money. At some point, the developer will be happy just to be able to satisfy his or her debt-related obligations to the lender. It is at this point that price concessions are frequently made, especially to an all-cash buyer. In many cases, these concessions can be quite significant.

As a builder, I'm constantly on the lookout for distressed developers who may be able to offer lots to me on a discounted basis. My first experience with a distressed developer occurred in the late 1980s in the Houston area. During that period of time, the real estate market was practically dead due to the recent savings and loan crisis. The developer, who had already sold about 75 percent of the lots, discovered that his sales activity had almost come to a complete standstill. I agreed to purchase three large adjoining lots from him for well under their market value. I then subdivided the three lots into four slightly smaller lots, kept the best one for myself, and sold the other three!

On another more recent occasion, I came across a community that was only about three years old. The original builder there apparently ran into financial difficulty that caused the progress of new home construction to come to a complete halt. The developer of the subdivision had tried unsuccessfully for over six months to get another builder to come in and take over where the previous builder had left off. This put the developer in a situation in which he became very anxious to sell the lots. I agreed to purchase the remaining 28 lots from him at a discounted price under very favorable terms. This gave Symphony Homes the ability to offer a more competitively priced product in that particular market.

Opportunities to purchase lots from distressed developers vary from region to region. As a real estate investor, your interest most likely lies in purchasing houses rather than vacant land. I would nevertheless caution you *not* to overlook this very viable and profitable method of purchasing undervalued property. Even if you choose not to build a house on it, you can still resell the land at a later date—oftentimes for a very handsome profit.

Distressed Builders

Like developers, builders face a variety of challenges on a daily basis. The lifeblood of any business is cash. The ability to manage that cash is essential and can mean the difference between success and failure. This is especially true of projects that require tens of thousands of dollars to build, such as houses. A builder who may be working on 10, 20, or even 50 houses at a time must maintain a delicate balance between the company's cash inflows and its cash outflows. Any number of unforeseen factors can upset this delicate balance. For example, builders use a variety of raw materials in the construction of new homes, including steel, lumber, and copper. An increase in price in any one of these raw materials can have a significant adverse impact on a builder's gross margins, thereby eroding profits. If during the construction process builders find themselves short of cash to cover the higher prices, they may become distressed and subsequently forced to take some type of defensive action, such as selling at a discount to raise immediate cash. The cash flow situation will become increasingly worse if a builder does not find a way to overcome the imbalance between cash inflows and outflows.

One particular builder I know used to build houses in the same community that my company did. I had observed over the course of a year or so that the builder was seldom in the subdivision and that a building superintendent was rarely present. I often wondered about the quality of these homes, as well as the quality of the leadership and management skills employed there. One day, rumors began circulating that they had just declared bankruptcy. The rumors were confirmed a few days later by several of the trades that worked for them as well as a number of angry homeowners. At the time of filing for bankruptcy, the builder had several houses at various stages of completion. All work on them came to an abrupt halt until such time as the bankruptcy proceedings were concluded. The lender providing the construction financing was left with the uncompleted houses, which became available for sale at discounted prices to anyone who was interested. To my knowledge, the homes were eventually purchased by individuals wanting to save money by finishing the houses themselves. I was not interested in them at the time because of the incompatibility of the other builder's product line with that of our own.

Ideally, as an investor seeking to take advantage of a distressed builder's unfortunate circumstances, it is best if the houses can be purchased before the builder files for bankruptcy. Given a choice, most builders would rather work with buyers by offering strong price incentives than be forced into the otherwise inevitable failure of their companies. Purchasing properties of this type, however, does require a degree of specialized knowledge since the houses will be at various stages of construction. Unless you already have the skills necessary to properly assess the work required to complete a house, I recommend enlisting the help of a builder who can guide you through the process and also provide an accurate estimate of the cost required to finish building the house.

Distressed Home Buyers

Another good opportunity for finding undervalued properties results from those home buyers who become distressed in the process of purchasing a new home. Although buying a new home is supposed to be a very positive experience for people, unfortunately it doesn't always work out that way. Like developers and builders, home buyers have their own unique set of challenges to deal with. Sometimes these challenges are difficult to overcome and cause the buyers distress in one form or another. This distress can potentially lead to creating yet another opportunity for investors to purchase undervalued houses.

If you and your spouse have ever built a house, you know firsthand how much stress can be caused by trying to get everything done. Whether you're working with a builder or trying to build the house yourself, there can still be a tremendous amount of stress involved in the process. There are numerous tasks that must be completed in an expedient manner to bring about the successful completion of a new home. For example, financing and insurance must be obtained, a site must be selected, and decisions about floor plans must be made. That's just the beginning. Exterior selections for both type and color of roofing, siding, brick, stucco, windows, and landscaping, to name a few, must be made. Interior selections for flooring, paint, cabinets, appliances, bathroom fixtures, lighting and light switches, and electrical outlets are just the beginning. Okay, you have a bunch of stuff to pick out. So what's the big deal? First of all, the very fact that all of the responsibilities that go along with building a house, such as making numerous selections, can create stress. Furthermore, if two spouses are trying to pick things out together and there is a difference in their preferences, the level of stress in the relationship can quickly escalate. She wants hardwood floors in the kitchen; he wants ceramic tile. She wants white bay cabinets; he wants maple cabinets. She wants a jetted bath-tub; he wants an oversized shower enclosure. The list goes on and on. If these differences between them cannot be resolved peaceably, the result can be separation and even divorce. The house that was supposed to be the couple's dream home has instead become a nightmare. If the couple backs out of the purchase of their now partially completed home, the builder can potentially be stuck with a house that was supposed to be sold. The house moves from the builder's presold inventory to spec inventory. As we've already discussed, builders do not like to sit on specs for any length of time, especially one that was supposed to be sold. To move the house out of inventory, the builder will likely offer special incentives, or may even be willing to make price concessions.

Another situation that can arise when individuals or couples purchase new homes is not being able to sell their previous homes. In other words, before closing on a new house can occur, a buyer must first sell the house he or she is living in. When the new house is completed, builders typically have a firm closing date that they expect the buyer to adhere to. If the buyers have not sold the home they are moving from, they are suddenly faced with the prospect of making two house payments—for which they may not qualify. Most buyers typically qualify for only one house payment at a time. If they are suddenly faced with having to make two payments, the mortgage company that has prequalified them for the new house may be unwilling to extend credit to them until their existing house is sold.

Although the house the buyers are moving from is likely to be in fairly good condition, especially since they are trying to sell it, having to make two house payments may cause them to be willing to take considerably less than its true market value. As mentioned earlier, I found myself in that very position several years ago when my wife and I were required to close on our new house in Michigan before we had sold our house in Texas. After about six months of making payments on both houses, a buyer offered me much less than what similar houses in the neighborhood were selling for. I wasn't at all excited about taking less than what I thought the house was worth, but I was thankful for the opportunity to be relieved of the obligation to the mortgage company on the other residence.

Locating distressed buyers in a situation such as this can be a bit of a challenge, but the potential to save thousands of dollars on the purchase of a house makes the effort required to find them well worth it. One way to locate buyers who may be faced with making two payments is to have real estate agents do a search in the MLS for houses that are vacant. Oftentimes, the sellers of those houses have been relocated. If they have, there's a very good chance they are making dual house payments. Another way to locate distressed buyers who are faced with the prospect of making two house payments is to check with sales agents who staff a particular community. Although they are not at liberty to disclose personal information, the agents are generally aware of whether or not their buyers have sold their existing houses or not. Knowing that they have not sold their houses, the sales agent will gladly refer you to either the buyers or their sales agents. Doing so will increase the likelihood that the sales agents will be able to close their deals.

Introductory Sales

Many builders face another unique challenge in newly developed communities—trying to generate sales momentum. When a subdivision is first developed, it can be difficult to attract buyers into the new community. If the subdivision, for example, has room for a total of 100 home sites and there's only a model home and two or three houses in the entire community, it can be very difficult to attract home buyers to live there. This is because many people do not want to be the first ones to move into a new community. There are several reasons for this. One reason is that families with children typically want to move into a neighborhood environment where there are other children to play with. If there are only a handful of houses in the neighborhood, their kids won't have any other kids to play with. Another reason is that it can sometimes take several years to build out an entire community. In this situation, the families already residing there must be tolerant of the constant construction taking place. This means listening to the sound of hammers, nail guns, and heavy equipment day after day, as well as driving on streets that sometimes have mud, debris, and even nails on them. Finally, new communities often have very few trees and landscaping. As a result, some people prefer to live in established neighborhoods where the trees are grown and mature and where vegetation flourishes in abundance.

The builder's challenge is to get as many people in as short a period of time as possible to move into a new community. Because of the high carrying costs in both interest and taxes on an entire subdivision, builders must be aggressive in doing whatever they can to generate sales. If a builder's initial sales are slow, he or she will barely be able to cover the carrying costs, much less make a profit. Like any other industry, builders are in business to make money. If they can't generate a decent return on their invested capital, they may as well leave their money in the bank and go to work for someone else.

In an effort to generate sales momentum, builders often do several things. One of the first things they like to do is to begin construction on several spec houses. The term *spec* is used to refer to houses a builder constructs on a *speculative* basis; thus, the word *spec* is short for speculative. It's important for the builder to show as much activity in the new community as possible. Doing so creates excitement and gives potential buyers the impression that there is a lot of interest in the area and that homes are selling fast. New home buyers like to see activity because it is reassuring to them in the sense that they are not alone in their decision to purchase in a particular area. They tell themselves, "If other people are buying houses here, then it must be okay for us to buy one too." On the other hand, if a community appears to be stagnant with very little or no construction activity, it appears that no one is interested in moving into the area. Buyers ask themselves, "If no one else is building a house here, why should we?" The more specs the builder puts up, the more excitement it creates; the more excitement it creates, the more houses he or she sells. Once the specs start going up, additional sales such as "presales" or "build-to-suits" will occur. As the builder begins these new houses, even more construction begins, which also helps to create momentum.

During this initial start-up phase, builders often offer all kinds of incentives to jump-start new sales activity. For example, they may offer a $5,000 free-landscaping package, or perhaps include a free-appliance package. Some builders will hold a "one-weekend-only sale" at which time they agree to throw in any number of free options and upgrades provided the purchaser buys that weekend. Additionally, some builders may even be willing to negotiate with prospective buyers on price just to get a sale. I've had buyers come in on many occasions and ask for price concessions. Although I don't get overly excited about giving away the company's profits, I am willing to work with buyers to some degree in an effort to get houses sold. With each house that is sold, builders reduce their carrying costs and get that much closer to being able to operate at a level that is profitable.

Finally, builders typically offer low introductory prices in newly developed communities to generate sales momentum. Buyers who take advantage of these lower prices will usually enjoy the greatest price appreciation in the subdivision. Once the new home sales increase to a level that is acceptable to the builder, a series of price increases will be implemented. As the new home prices increase, so do the values of the homes previously built. Don't be afraid to be one of the first home buyers in a new community. Instead, take advantage of any price concessions or promotional incentives that may be available, as well as equity buildup through a series of price increases.

Excess Inventory

Builders who have overestimated their respective market's ability to absorb specs are another source for locating undervalued properties.

Carrying costs, which include interest, taxes, insurance, utilities, and possibly lawn care, can quickly eat into a builder's profits. The longer builders carry a spec in inventory, the more it costs them. At some point they must weigh the cost of carrying the house in inventory against the cost of reducing its price. If a builder hasn't had an offer on a particular spec in several months, she or he will likely be anxious to entertain most any offer.

As a builder, our company finds itself with excess inventory from time to time. One recent example that comes to mind is a house that was originally priced at $246,900. After several months of sitting on the market with no offers yet received, we lowered the price to $239,900. The house then sat for several more months on the market, still with no offers. Our sales agents had shown the house to a number of prospective buyers, but none of them liked it well enough to purchase it. This particular house happened to back up to an older neighborhood that looked in places more like a junkyard than a residential community. Although we erected a six-foot cedar fence to help obstruct the view, the junky backyards of the neighbors could still be seen from the upstairs bedrooms of the house. We finally had one couple who liked the house well enough to at least make an offer on it. Their offering price of $230,000 for the house was almost $10,000 below our asking price of $239,900. We countered at $235,900, which they accepted, provided we agreed to pay $2,900 of their closing costs. This made the effective selling price of the home $233,000. Recall that the house was originally priced at $246,900. Although I wasn't overly pleased about an offer that was almost $17,000 under our original asking price, I decided to accept it to get the house out of inventory. The benefits of doing so meant transferring the carrying costs of the home to the new owners and also freeing up some of our cash that was tied up in the property.

In this situation, the couple who purchased the house got a great deal on their beautiful new home. If they had come to us and asked us to custom build the same house for them, there would have been very little, if any, price incentives. As you drive through newer residential communities, be on the lookout for homes that look as if they have been sitting vacant for a while. As you identify these potential opportunities, there's a good chance that you may be able to purchase one at a significant discount.

Final Closeout Sales

Another terrific way of finding undervalued properties is by looking for newly developed subdivisions that are in their last phase of construction and have only one or two houses available. In this situation, builders often hold final closeout sales and offer special incentives to unload any remaining inventory. This phase of a community is at the opposite end of its development life cycle. Rather than trying to create excitement and generate momentum, builders are instead winding down their operations and moving on to the next project. By this phase of development, the builder's model home has typically already been sold and the sales agents have moved on to the new community. Rather than exert time and energy selling the last of the available inventory, the builder and his staff are instead focusing on generating sales activity in the new community. As a result, they will often lower the price of the last few houses in order to sell them quickly.

I have a sales agent who recently purchased a new home using this very strategy. Just before she came to work for me, she had located a brand new home in a very nice community. As it turns out, the builder had already moved on to the next project and had one remaining house for sale in this subdivision. Several families had expressed an interest in the home, but none had made an offer on it yet. The builder decided to reduce the price by $20,000 and then instructed his staff to contact any families who might be interested in it. The very next day, my sales agent happened to be in the community and saw the house for sale. She contacted the sales agent who informed her that the builder had lowered the price the day before by $20,000 to get the house sold. My sales agent, who bought it on the spot, was able to enjoy the benefit of substantial equity built into the price of her new home!

High-Growth Markets

Several regions throughout the country have enjoyed rapid growth over the last few years. These areas are predominantly located where the climate is warmer, such as the Southeast, South, and Southwest. For example, according to the Bureau of the Census, Atlanta ranked number one in the nation, issuing in excess of 53,000 building permits for new home starts in 2003 alone. Phoenix, Riverside, Houston, and Washington, D.C., rounded out the top five, adding an additional 147,000 new home starts. Table 7.1 illustrates the top 25 housing markets for 2003 in terms of new construction starts.

In several of these high-growth markets, houses are sold almost the day they are put on the market. In Las Vegas, Nevada, for example, the average number of residents moving into the metropolitan area each month is over 5,000. Imagine 5,000 people moving into your city each and every month, month after month, and the demand it would place on housing. With a strong demand and limited supply, prices have only one way to go—up. The median price of an existing home sold in Las Vegas in October 2003 was $174,000. That's $24,000 more than the same month in 2002. That equates to an annual increase of 16 percent. New home prices increased at almost the same pace. The median price during the same period for a new home was $208,124, while just a year earlier it was $184,159. That equates to an annual increase of 13 percent. In some areas, price increases approached 20 percent due to their preferred location and the amenities offered in some communities. Rates of return like these are pretty hard to beat, especially when the return is calculated based on the actual down payment.

It also has been reported in some regions that builders can barely keep pace with the demand for new housing. Demand is so great, in

Table 7.1   Metro Areas Ranked by Number of Single-Family Permits Issued in 2003

Rank	Metro Area	Number of Permits
1	Atlanta	53,753
2	Phoenix-Mesa	46,591
3	Riverside-San Bernardino	35,733
4	Houston	33,965
5	Washington, D.C.	30,755
6	Chicago	30,733
7	Las Vegas	30,278
8	Dallas	26,905
9	Orlando	22,385
10	Minneapolis-St. Paul	20,327
11	Tampa-St. Petersburg	20,179
12	Charlotte-Gastonia-Rock Hill	17,155
13	Sacramento	17,126
14	Detroit	15,328
15	Raleigh-Durham-Chapel Hill	14,072
16	Ft. Worth-Arlington	13,904
17	Indianapolis	13,062
18	Denver	13,005
19	Jacksonville	12,637
20	Philadelphia	12,406
21	St. Louis	11,954
22	Columbus, OH	11,693
23	Kansas City	11,661
24	Nashville	11,471
25	Seattle-Bellevue-Everett	11,226

fact, that lotto systems are used to determine which buyers will be eligible to purchase a new home. With the demand for housing so strong and the supply so limited, it doesn't seem possible that any houses could be undervalued. The irony in a situation such as this is that by the time the builder begins construction of a new house, obtains the appropriate permits, and works for the next six months or so to complete it, home prices have already risen by several percent. Consider the increase of 13 percent experienced by residents of Las Vegas. By the time a builder started construction of a new house and finished it six months later, the price of the new home rose on average almost 7 percent! If the builder sells a house today for $200,000, that same house will be worth $214,000 in six months. That's a remarkable rate of appreciation not only for the housing market, but for any asset class. In a strong market such as this, what may not be undervalued today surely will be considered undervalued six months or one year from now.

I know a well-respected real estate investor who routinely invests in various markets throughout the nation. Las Vegas is one of them. He recently partnered with a builder who was just beginning the initial phases of construction in a new subdivision. The investor agreed to purchase 50 houses from the builder at today's prices and gave him a $5,000 down payment for each of the 50 houses for a total of $250,000. Since the builder had 50 houses under contract, he was able to take the contracts to his lender for financing and begin construction of the new houses immediately. The investor, meanwhile, teamed up with a local real estate firm to begin marketing the new houses at a price adjusted for 6 to 18 months worth of appreciation since that's how long it would take to complete the project. If the average price of each house increases $25,000, the real estate investor will enjoy a lucrative rate of return of 500 percent! While the ability to take advantage of opportunities such as this is limited to those markets experiencing a rapid rate of growth, they are nevertheless available to those investors astute enough to recognize and participate in them.

Undervalued Opportunities in New Construction

If you're interested in buying a new home, don't overlook these potential opportunities to find an undervalued house. Developers, builders, and even other new home buyers face a variety of challenges that can cause them distress. Additionally, price incentives are typically offered to the first buyers moving into a new community, on excess inventory held by builders, and during the final closeout of a community. Finally, in high-growth areas where prices are increasing daily, what may not be considered undervalued today surely will be six months or a year from now.

8

Five Ways to Unlock Hidden Value through Changes in Use

In the last chapter, we explored seven different methods of finding undervalued properties that were all related to some form of new construction, building, or development activity. These methods represent seven additional tools that can be stored in your memory, where they will always be available for immediate recall and ready to use at a moment's notice. In this chapter, we'll examine the effects that a change in use of a particular piece of property can have on its value. For a property being maintained for its current use, for instance, this may not necessarily be its highest and best use at present. For example, in the case of a house built 50 years ago in what was once a residential area that has since given way to commercial development, it may be that converting it from its current use as single-family residential to commercial use would add value to it over and above its value as a house. The notion that value can sometimes be created by simply converting real estate from one use to another has been demonstrated time and time again. This notion holds true because of the way that value is measured. In Chapter 2 we discussed the three primary methods of determining the value of a property, which are the replacement cost method, income capitalization method, and the sales comparison method. By understanding the true nature and function of each of these three methods, an investor can maximize the respective applicability to a given situation. For example, to measure the value of a single-family house, the comparable sales method is the most appropriate appraisal method. However, if the house were converted to some type of commercial space, the income capitalization method would become the preferred appraisal method. Each of these two methods would very likely yield different results. The wise investor who knows how to apply the appropriate valuation methods described herein will most certainly have the advantage over other investors.

To discover oftentimes latent opportunities in real estate that can be unlocked by a change in use, investors must first be aware that such possibilities exist. They must then learn how to recognize them and convert or change their usage so as to maximize the value inherent within them. Change in use opportunities may lie dormant for many years until such time as an investor comes along and discovers another use for a particular piece of real estate. While there are innumerable ways to unlock the hidden value in real estate, in this chapter we'll focus on five of the more common ways (see Figure 8.1). These methods include converting single-family houses into commercial office space, multifamily rentals, and condominiums. We'll also discuss converting multifamily apartments and commercial real estate into condominiums.

Single Family to Commercial Office

In *The Complete Guide to Real Estate Finance: How to Analyze Any Single Family, Multifamily, or Commercial Property* (New Jersey: John

**Five Ways to Unlock Hidden Value
through Changes in Use**

1. Single family to commercial office
2. Single family to multifamily
3. Commercial to condominium
4. Multifamily to condominium
5. Single family to condominium

Figure 8.1

Wiley & Sons, 2004), I used the example discussed in this section to examine the conversion of a single-family residence to one of commercial office space. This example will help demonstrate how to apply two different appraisal methods: the sales comparison method and the income capitalization method. The single-family house in this example is one that I purchased for the purpose of converting it to office space for my company. At the time, I was looking for the most cost-effective way of opening a new office without paying the higher commercial rates that were common in this particular area. I also preferred to own a building rather than to lease space. This would give me more control of the premises and would also provide me with several of the benefits of owning real estate discussed in Chapter 1. Over time, the building would appreciate in value, provide a generous tax savings through depreciation, and enjoy a reduction in principal of the loan balance.

This is why understanding the differences among the three market valuation methods is so important. If you can grasp the underlying logic and understand the fundamental principles of each method, you can use them to your advantage to create value. Because this was a single-family house, the most appropriate valuation method was to use the comparable sales approach. This is the method the appraiser used when he came out to appraise the property. He examined other properties similar to the subject property and made adjustments as necessary to derive a value that was most appropriate for the property in its state of use as a residence. Now that the house has been converted to an income-producing office building, its usage has changed from residential to commercial. The value of the building is no longer based upon comparable sales of similar houses. It is instead based on the income produced from its rents. As we've already learned, the income capitalization method is the most appropriate method of valuing a property such as this.

So there you have it. In my attempt to identify a less expensive alternative to leasing commercial office space, I was able to locate a property that was well suited for the use I intended and in an ideal location for an office building. The high traffic location was especially appealing because it enables our company, Symphony Homes, to greatly increase its brand identity and name recognition in that particular community. With 22,000 motorists driving by our brightly lit sign each day, they become more and more familiar with our name. By sheer virtue of our presence, many of them have and will continue to seek our services. With 2,400 square feet of space, the building is large enough to meet our current needs. Furthermore, it is a much cheaper alternative to leasing office or retail space in the same area, and certainly much cheaper than purchasing office or retail space. The most important concept to understand in this example is that by converting a single-family house into commercial office space, I was able to create value where it did not exist before. Just as having a comprehensive understanding of the different valuation methods enabled me to create value in this situation, it can enable you to do the same in similar situations. I cannot overemphasize the importance of familiarizing yourself with and understanding these methods. The key to your success in real estate is understanding value!

Single Family to Multifamily

Another way of adding value to a property is by converting it from a single-family dwelling to a multifamily dwelling. For example, a 1,500-square-foot single-family dwelling may rent for $1,500 per month, but if that same dwelling were converted into three smaller units that rented for $600 per month each, the total revenue would be increased by $300, or 20 percent. This concept works especially well in areas close to colleges and universities where student housing is in high demand. Most students right out of high school are single. Their primary criterion for housing is "cheap." I know of one neighborhood in particular where most of the houses were built 50 to 60 years ago as single-family dwellings. About 20 years ago, a well-known university opened a satellite campus just down the street from the neighborhood. Many of the houses in that area have since been converted to accommodate the students needing affordable housing. Because they are income-producing properties, their values have increased to reflect the market rates for similar types of property.

Converting a single-family property into a multifamily property such as a duplex or triplex can be done in a variety of ways. In the previous section, I described how I converted a single-family house into commercial office space. What I did not mention, however, is that at some time in the history of that century-old house, it had been used as a multifamily dwelling. In the rear of the house, a private stairway had been built to access a smaller one-bedroom efficiency unit, complete with kitchenette, bathroom, and bedroom, that was situated above the main living area of the house. The unit was separated from the rest of the house by a wall that had been erected in the upstairs hallway. So, while the main portion of the house was accessed through either the front or the side doors, the efficiency unit was accessed only through the rear stairwell. This allowed the two families sharing the house to come and go without disturbing each other. It just so happens that the building next to this one was also converted once upon a time from a single-family house into a smaller, multifamily property. This particular dwelling, however, had been converted to accommodate three families rather than two.

The primary issue you must be aware of when considering this type of conversion, as with any conversion, is to determine whether or not the local governing bodies will allow it. In other words, you can't just buy a house, put in some walls to create two or more distinct units, and expect to rent it out. Permission is generally required by the governing bodies that oversee zoning and building ordinances in the area the property is located in. This authority typically lies with the local zoning board of appeals or the planning commission. If a precedent has already been set in the area by another property that has previously been converted, then the case can be made that the property you are considering should also be granted permission. A word of caution: if you think you can make this kind of change without any of the neighbors noticing, think again. A good friend of mine who owned a large home in a lavish neighborhood once attempted to rent one of the bedrooms to a tenant. He didn't make any structural changes to the house, but was merely attempting to lease one of the rooms out. The neighbors got wind of his intent to lease a room out and quickly contacted an attorney. My friend was sent a strongly worded letter citing that strict adherence to the definition of "single-family housing" was required and that residents in the neighborhood would not tolerate unrelated third parties sharing a dwelling that was so designated. In my opinion, the neighbors were a bit on the snooty side and should have minded their own business. I believe this extreme example borders on infringing upon an owner's property rights.

Commercial to Condominium

The activities required to convert a building into one of common ownership whereby units are deeded separately and owned individually lie at the very core of the condominium conversion process. Purchasers of condominium units buy an "undivided interest" in the common elements of the building or development. Common elements generally include the land the building is situated on, lobby areas, public halls, driveways, access roads, and parking areas. Other common areas include the exterior components of the building such as siding and brick, as well as the electrical, plumbing, and heating and air-conditioning systems that service the building. Instead of owning shares in a cooperative corporation, condominium buyers own their individual units outright and receive deeds for them. Each of the condominium owners is responsible for paying a proportionate share of the building's utility costs, related employee salaries, and other expenses of operation that are common to all of the owners. Furthermore, each condominium owner pays real estate taxes, which are separately assessed against each unit, as well as the cost of any mortgage obtained to finance the original purchase. Like owners of single-family houses, condominium owners can deduct mortgage interest and tax payments for income tax purposes. Condominium units are typically governed by a board of managers elected by the unit owners. The board's authority to operate the building is explained in detail in the condominium declaration and bylaws, a copy of which is included in the offering plan. These documents provide rules and procedures for conducting the affairs of the condominium as well as defining the rights and obligations of the unit owners. The bylaws, for example, may limit the right of the individual unit owners to make certain types of changes or modifications to their units, especially to the exterior portion of them. They may also prohibit unit owners from leasing the units out as rentals. Because the laws that govern condominium conversions can be somewhat complex and vary by state, you will most likely need the legal assistance of an experienced attorney when preparing the requisite documents. Take a moment to review the condominium conversion guide in Figure 8.2, which was prepared for tenants, prospective buyers, and owners in the city of Seattle.

Seattle Department of Planning and Development
— formerly the Department of Design, Construction and Land Use

CAM 602

client assistance memo

Condominium Conversion: A Guide for Tenants, Prospective Buyers and Owners

April 2003

The conversion of apartments to condominiums is governed both by Washington state laws and by Seattle ordinance. State law gives tenants the chance to buy their own unit, and assures that all buyers are informed of the responsibilities and costs they incur when they purchase a condominium. State law also insures that tenants receive notice of the conversion, and the chance to buy their unit, at least 90 days before they can be required to move.

If you own property that you are considering converting, you should review the state Horizontal Property Regimes Act (Revised Code of Washington [R.C.W.] 64.32) and the Condominium Conversion Act (R.C.W. 64.34) for detailed state requirements.

Seattle's Condominium Conversion Ordinance (Seattle Municipal Code, Chapter 22.903) requires condominium developers to provide financial help to eligible renters who are forced to move when their apartments are converted to condominiums. It also requires that the building be inspected for defects before any units can be sold.

The Condominium Conversion Ordinance is administered by DPD's Compliance Service Center, located on the 19th floor of Seattle Municipal Tower at 700 Fifth Avenue, (206) 615-0808.

TENANT PROTECTION

When are tenants notified that their building is being converted to condominiums?

State law requires landlords to notify tenants of a condominium conversion at least 90 days before a tenant can be required to vacate. The owner or developer must notify tenants which units are for sale, and must give them certain financial disclosures specified in state law concerning purchasing and owning a unit.

Project developers may file a declaration of conversion with the King County Records Division either before or after offering units for sale. In some cases, the filing of a declaration may occur months before any units are offered for sale. Regardless of when the declaration was filed, a tenant must receive written notice of the conversion and the offer to buy his or her own unit at least 90 days before he or she can be required to move.

For details on tenants' rights under the State Condominium Conversion Act, please consult R.C.W. 64.34.

How long may tenants occupy their apartments once they have received the notice of conversion?

Tenants have a right to stay at least 90 days after receiving notice of the conversion. The owner may require tenants to move at the end of the 90-day period or may prefer to continue renting until the units have sold.

If the notice of conversion specifies that a unit must be vacated at the end of the 90-day period, then the tenant must move out by that date. If no specific requirement to move is stated, then the tenant does not have to move until the owner issues a written termination of tenancy notice.

Who receives relocation assistance? How much is it?

After giving the 90-day notice, developers must pay $500 to eligible tenants who move out and do not buy their unit. This relocation assistance should be paid on

www.seattle.gov/dpd

City of Seattle
Department of Planning & Development
Gregory J. Nickels, Mayor   Diane Sugimura, Director

700 5th Avenue, Suite 2000
P.O. Box 34019
Seattle, WA 98124-4019
(206) 684-8600

Printed on totally chlorine free paper made with 100% post-consumer fiber

Figure 8.2   Condo Guide for Seattle Residents

Five Ways to Unlock Hidden Value through Changes in Use

or before the date the tenant vacates the unit. To be eligible, a tenant household must earn less than 80% of the median income of Seattle, for a household of a given size. Income limits are as follows:

Household Size	Maximum Monthly Income
1 person	$3,175
2 persons	$3,625
3 persons	$4,079
4 persons	$4,533
5 persons	$4,896
6 persons	$5,258
7 persons	$5,621
8 persons	$5,983

These figures change periodically. To verify current eligibility limits, please contact DPD's Compliance Service Center at (206) 615-0808.

Eligible tenants who vacate their apartment any time after receiving the 90-day notice must be paid relocation assistance. The relocation assistance payment is in addition to damage deposits or other refunds to which the tenant is entitled. The landlord may, however, deduct unpaid rent or other amounts owed by the tenant from the relocation assistance. It may be necessary for the landlord to document these charges.

What protection do tenants have from being evicted before and during the conversion process?

Under state law, during the 90-day notice period tenants may be evicted only for the following three reasons:

- Failure to pay rent;

- Conduct that disturbs other tenants' peaceful enjoyment of the premises; and

- Causing waste or damage, or creating a nuisance.

These reasons are more limited than those allowed by Seattle's Just Cause Eviction Ordinance. In addition, during the 90-day notice period, state law does not allow the terms of tenancy, including the amount of rent, to be changed. (See CAM 604: *Seattle Laws on Property Owner and Tenant Rights and Responsibilities* for more information on the Just Cause Eviction Ordinance.)

BUYER PROTECTION

What assurance do buyers have that the building is in good condition?

Seattle's Condominium Conversion Ordinance requires that the owner have the property inspected for compliance with Housing Code requirements by the DPD Inspection Services Division. This must be done before the owner delivers any offering statement or condominium conversion notice to tenants. All Housing Code violations **must** be corrected at least seven days before the first closing of the sale of a unit, or by the compliance date stated in any Notice of Violation issued as a result of the inspection, whichever is sooner. The inspection report must be delivered to all prospective purchasers, including tenants, along with the public offering statement and the condominium conversion notice.

What guarantees do new owners have that major repairs won't be needed immediately?

For a period of one year, developers must warrant all repairs and improvements made to correct code violations revealed by the Housing Code inspection. City law requires that the developer establish an escrow fund for this purpose within thirty days after the first sale of a unit. The amount in this fund should be ten percent of the cost of the repairs and improvements that were needed to bring the property into compliance with the Housing Code. If repairs are needed after a unit is purchased, escrow funds can be used to pay for such repairs only after the developer has been advised in writing of a problem and has failed to complete repairs in a reasonable time. Even if the escrow fund is used entirely, the developer may still be liable for repairs. Any money remaining in the fund after one year is returned to the developer.

Figure 8.2 (*continued*)   Condo Guide for Seattle Residents

How to Find Undervalued Properties

CONDOMINIUM CONVERSION PROCEDURES

Developers unfamiliar with the city's Condominium Conversion Ordinance should contact the DPD Compliance Service Center at (206) 615-0808 to review city requirements. In addition, developers should review state requirements (R.C.W. 64.32 and 64.34). The following is a brief summary of some of the details of converting rental housing to condominiums:

Filing a declaration: The developer may initiate the conversion process by filing a declaration to convert pursuant to the Horizontal Property Regimes Act (R.C.W. 64.32) with the King County Records and Elections Office. (206) 296-5117.

Housing Code inspection: Before offering any units for sale, the developer must have the entire premises subject to conversion inspected by a City of Seattle housing code inspector. The inspection is scheduled after the developer fills out an inspection request form and returns it with the required inspection fee. DPD is required to make the inspection within 45 days of the request. Checks should be made payable to the City of Seattle. Forms and fee information are attached to this Client Assistance Memo. For more information call the Compliance Service Center at (206) 615-0808.

Required repairs: The developer will receive a written inspection report within 14 days of completion of the inspection. The inspection will cover the major systems and components of the building, including shelter, heating, electrical systems, fire safety, and security. If no violations are discovered, a certificate indicating no repairs are required will be issued. If violations are discovered, the report will be titled "Notice of Violation" and will list items that need to be brought into compliance with the Code.

All of the Housing Code violations revealed by the inspection must be corrected at least seven days prior to the first closing of the sale of any unit or by the compliance date on the inspection report (Notice of Violation), whichever is sooner. Corrections are required even if the developer decides not to complete the conversion process. Once the corrections are completed, a Certificate of Repairs will be issued by DPD.

Offering units for sale: The developer may begin offering the units to the tenants after receiving the Housing Code inspection report. The following is a partial list of disclosures that must be given to tenants and other prospective buyers. Developers planning a conversion should consult the State Condominium Act

(RCW 64.34) for complete details about these and other requirements.

- The Notice of Condominium Conversion and public offering statement, and a copy of the written inspection report. A copy of the Certificate of Repairs must be given to the purchaser before the closing of any sale;

- Copies of documents the owner has filed with any governmental agency as required by the State Horizontal Property Regimes Act (R.C.W. 64.32);

- Itemization of repairs and improvements that were made during the six months prior to the offer of sale, and those that will be made prior to the close of sale;

- Statement of services and expenses paid by the building owner that will be terminated or transferred to unit owners;

- Estimates of the useful life of the building's major components and mechanical systems and of the cost to repair any which have a useful life of less than five years;

- Itemization of the monthly costs of owning each unit, including loan payments, taxes, insurance, utility costs, and other relevant expenses.

Relocation assistance: Condominium developers must pay $500 relocation assistance to an eligible tenant on or before the date the tenant vacates his unit. Developers should make allowances for this requirement in their financial planning.

Certifying required repairs: The developer may close the sale of an individual condominium unit only after all items listed on a Notice of Violation have been certified as corrected and after receipt of the Certificate of Repairs from DPD. The developer must give each purchaser a copy of the Certificate of Repairs at least seven days prior to the closing of the sale.

Warranty of required repairs: Within thirty days after the sale of the first unit, the developer must establish an escrow fund equal to ten percent of the cost of all warrantable repairs and improvements to the property. All repairs and improvements required by the Housing Code inspection are warrantable for one year. Location of the escrow fund must be made known to all condominium unit owners and to the owners' association.

Figure 8.2 (*continued*)   Condo Guide for Seattle Residents

Five Ways to Unlock Hidden Value through Changes in Use

INSPECTION FEES

Effective January 1, 2003, the fee for advisory inspections requested pursuant to the Housing and Building Maintenance Code—or for inspections required by the Condominium Conversion Ordinance—is charged at the rate of two and one-half (2.5) times the Base Fee for inspecting a building and one housing unit PLUS a charge at the rate of one-half (.5) times the Base Fee for inspecting each additional housing unit in the same building.

Examples

Sample fee calculations for **one building** with varying numbers of units:

1-Unit Fee:

2.5 x $150 (base fee) = $375

10-Unit Fee:

2.5 x $150 (base fee) + 9 additional units x $75 (0.5 base fee) = $1,050

20-Unit Fee:

2.5 x $150 (base fee) + 19 additional units x $75 (0.5 base fee) = $1,800

If there are **two buildings** each containing 10 units, then the fee for each building would be the 10-unit fee listed above times the number of buildings.

No additional fee will be charged for one follow-up inspection, if requested. If more inspections are required, the fee will be calculated at $150.00 for the first unit and $37.50 for each additional unit.

GETTING MORE INFORMATION

The Condominium Conversion Ordinance is available from the DPD Public Resource Center, located on the 20th floor of Seattle Municipal Tower at 700 Fifth Avenue, (206) 684-8467. It is also available on DPD's website at **www.seattle.gov/dpd/codes**.

If you have questions or need additional information, please contact the DPD Compliance Service Center at (206) 615-0808 or visit them on the 19th floor of Seattle Municipal Tower at 700 Fifth Avenue in downtown Seattle.

Access to Information

Links to electronic versions of DCLU **Client Assistance Memos (CAMs)** and other helpful publications are available on our website at **www.seattle.gov/dpd/publications**. Paper copies of these documents are available from our Public Resource Center, located on the 20th floor of Seattle Municipal Tower at 700 Fifth Avenue in downtown Seattle, (206) 684-8467.

Figure 8.2 (*continued*)   Condo Guide for Seattle Residents

Now that you have a better understanding of the condominium ownership concept, let's look at how other uses of land and buildings might be converted to serve this growing need. As the demand for housing continues to increase, so does the need for land and property that will accommodate tighter densities. With land becoming scarcer in certain metropolitan areas, developers and real estate investors have discovered innovative ways of meeting the increased demand for housing. One creative technique for meeting the housing demand is to convert existing commercial space into condominiums. In some high-tech areas where Americans once dominated the marketplace, for instance, engineering, manufacturing, and technology, jobs have been exported to other countries offering similar services but with a cheaper labor component. Although the initial impact of this mass exodus of jobs to overseas markets created an overabundance of commercial office space, property owners began seeking alternative uses for their buildings. By identifying population trends in the growth of their respective markets, property owners began filling the need for housing by converting existing commercial buildings to condominium units. Depending on the location and the specific needs of the marketplace, some commercial buildings have been converted into high-end luxury condos, while others have been converted into more affordable units. And, of course, the range between these two extremes runs the full gamut. Regardless of the specific price points of housing in a given area, the fact remains that the ability to convert unused and empty commercial building space into livable condominium units is very real.

Multifamily to Condominium

In this section, we'll examine the notion of converting a multifamily apartment building into individually owned condominium units. For those of you who may be unfamiliar with the way this process works, the basic idea is to convert individual units that are leased or rented out to tenants into units that are sold to homeowners. The purchaser of the condominium takes legal title to the unit and obtains an ownership interest in it that can then be sold or otherwise transferred if so desired. Certain legal steps must be taken before a conversion can be made. I recommend working with an attorney who has direct experience doing this rather than wasting your time by using an attorney who only practices general real estate law. Although the experienced attorney may charge a higher rate, you'll save several months of time using his or her services. In some instances, approvals may also be required from the city planning commission or board of zoning appeals before the conversion can take place. Your attorney or the local governmental body you are working with will be able to determine what specific steps need to be taken. If you haven't been involved in a multifamily to condominium conversion before, don't allow yourself to be intimidated at the prospect of doing so, because condo conversions can be very profitable. I wouldn't want to see any readers shortchange themselves just because they hadn't been through the conversion process before.

The property in this example was a 24-unit apartment building that happened to have some additional land that would accommodate another 80 units. The primary criteria I used to evaluate this project were based on its ability to generate an acceptable rate of return on a stand-alone basis. In other words, although the property could support the construction of another 80 units, I based its value on the ability to generate income as it currently existed. At the time I evaluated this opportunity, I had no interest in building the additional condominium units because I had not yet entered into the construction business. My analysis then was based on the value of the units only, since the land was of no additional value to me at that time. I should mention that my approach today would certainly be different because we build single-family housing units from the ground up during the normal course of our business activities.

The property was first brought to my attention by a real estate broker I had been working with for some time. Before ever going to look at a property, I make it a habit to review the related financial statements. If the deal makes sense after running it through one of the proprietary financial models I have developed, it may be worth taking a look at. In this case, the output from my model indicated that the returns based on the asking price of a little more than $1.5 million were inadequate. I decided, however, that it was still worth taking a look at it to see if there was a way that I could add or create value and also to get direct feedback from the seller to determine if there was some flexibility in his asking price. A few days later, I met with the broker, the seller, and a prospective property manager at the apartment building. My first impression of the property was that although it was off the beaten path, it appeared to be fairly well maintained. According to the seller, he had no problem keeping it rented. This statement, however, was inconsistent with the fact that he had two units that had been empty for over a month. Both the broker and the seller did their best to sell me on the property's upside potential with the construction of additional units and neither seemed to be too flexible on the asking price. I asked them both, "If developing the additional units is such a good opportunity, why isn't the seller doing that?" The seller responded that he "just wanted to sell the property" so he could retire. I've heard the "retire" reason for selling more times than I care to count. I think that when sellers use that term, what they really mean is they are "tired" of fooling with the management of their property.

In this example, because the property was not earning enough income to provide an acceptable rate of return operating as an apartment building, I decided not to buy it. In retrospect, however, if I had the construction experience then that I have now, I would have looked at it through an entirely different set of lenses. I have since developed a financial model that allows me to estimate construction costs and is, consequently, much better suited for this type of analysis. Following is a brief summary of what the potential profit in this deal might have looked like.

Cost Estimates:

Total Cost	$1,500,000
Number of Units	24
Average Cost per Unit	$62,500
Estimated Cost of Repairs	$20,000
Total Cost per Unit	$82,500

Revenue Estimates:

Estimated Resell Price	$110,000
Total Cost per Unit	$82,500
Gross Profit per Unit	$27,500
Number of Units	24
Total Gross Profit	$660,000

As you can see from this brief analysis, the opportunity to profit in this multifamily-to-condominium conversion was substantial. This analysis does not even include the profit from the additional 80 units that could have been built. An average profit of $20,000 per unit would have yielded another $1.6 million, bringing the total to $2.26 million. My inability to capitalize on the potential profits waiting to be unlocked in this conversion opportunity was a direct result of my lack of experience at the time. I hope those of you who find similar opportunities such as the one described here will not make the same mistake I did, but will instead jump at the chance to lock in over $2 million in profits!

Single Family to Condominium

In previous sections of this chapter, we discussed the possibility of converting a commercial property into a condominium property and then examined the possibility of converting a multifamily property into a condominium property. In this section, I'll share one of my favorite stories with you as we discuss the process of converting a single-family property into a condominium property. You'll learn how it's possible to get a free boat slip on prime lakefront property and make $380,000 doing so as I describe this exciting process! In *The Complete Guide to Investing in Rental Properties* (New York: McGraw Hill, 2004), I used the example discussed in this section to analyze the conversion of a single-family residence into nine condominium units.

The property in this example is an actual investment opportunity I purchased that came about as a result of my looking for an inexpensive place to dock my boat (which, incidentally, I didn't even own at the time). The single-family house described here was located directly across the street from a beautiful all sports lake in Lake Orion, Michigan. The property was not considered to be "lakefront," but rather "lakeview." While houses that are lakefront typically sell for $200 per square foot and up, houses that are lakeview sell for between $120 and $140 per square foot. The subject property falls into the second category with a couple of exceptions, which was the reason I became interested in it to begin with. The house sits directly across the street from the lake on a little over three-quarters of an acre and happens to be the only parcel of land uniquely situated with buildable lot space that is zoned Residential Multiple, or RM. So, although the property had only been used to build a single-family house, the land was large enough to accommodate several units. Before proceeding any further with this example, allow me to take a moment to provide you with the circumstances that brought about this rather unusual acquisition.

Shortly after writing the previous excerpt, I completed the purchase of the subject property, boat slips and all! The primary pieces needed to convert this property from single-family residential into multifamily condominium units were already in place. First, since the property was already zoned RM, no zoning changes would be required. This was especially important because having land or property rezoned can be a very costly and lengthy process, sometimes taking as long as several years, and even then there are no guarantees that the zoning request will be approved. Second, a review of the allowable density requirements as contained in the local ordinances suggested that between 8 and 10 units could be built, depending on their size. And, finally, I wanted the two boat slips that came with the deal for personal use, especially since they were already deeded separately from the main parcel. Another benefit of this particular deal was that income could be generated from the existing house on the property by renting it out. Although the rental income from the house would not be enough to cover all of the property's debt obligations, it would certainly help offset them during the approval period, which at the time was estimated to be several months. One additional benefit in this transaction was that the house on the property happened to be modular construction, which means that it could be disassembled and moved to another lot somewhere else just before construction on the condominiums began. Selling the house to a third party to move to another location would allow us to recoup some of the project's costs.

Since this project was approved just recently by the local planning commission, my company has not yet started construction on it. Our architects are in the process of completing the construction drawings that will be submitted along with the final engineering drawings later this month to the building department for final approval. As soon as the building permits are ready, we will begin construction on the nine condominium units and three boat storage units that were approved by the planning commission. In this example, the culmination of three unique factors gave birth to an opportunity that may otherwise never have come to life had I not been in the habit of exploring alternative possibilities for changes in land use. First, the fact that this parcel of land was already zoned RM naturally facilitated the construction of condominium units. Second, the fact that the parcel of land was large enough to accommodate several units provided ample profitability in a project of this size. Finally, my willingness to examine this opportunity from another perspective resulted in the birth of a project that will soon prove to be quite profitable and yield a handsome profit for my company, Symphony Homes. Net proceeds from this transaction are projected to be $380,000 and two boat slips on prime waterfront property!

To summarize, in this chapter we have demonstrated by providing several examples the idea that value can be created by converting real estate from one use to another. By learning when and how to use the most appropriate of the three primary methods of measuring real estate value, the prudent investor can exploit opportunities that would likely go undetected by other investors. Hidden opportunities in real estate can be unlocked by a change in use, but investors must be schooled in the art of detecting them. Such potential opportunities may lie dormant for many years. It is only when the investor who is willing to "look outside of the box" is able to discover another use for a particular piece of property. Although there are many ways to unlock the hidden value in real estate, five of the more common ways discussed in this chapter centered around converting a single-family house into either commercial office space, multifamily rentals, or condominium units, as well as converting multifamily apartments and commercial real estate into condominiums.

9

How to Find Undervalued Properties the Autopilot Way

In the last chapter, we examined five different methods for unlocking value through changes in the use of a property. By being constantly on the lookout for alternative uses for a property, investors can capitalize on conversion opportunities that will maximize its usage. Although adopting conversion practices such as the ones described are available to anyone, it is the vigilant investor who understands how to unlock value through changes in use that will be successful. In this chapter, we will explore several methods for finding undervalued properties automatically (see Figure 9.1). In other words, once you have taken the initial steps of building an "undervalued properties pipeline," you will enjoy a steady flow of opportunities that are just waiting for you to take

How to Find Undervalued Properties the Autopilot Way

1. Use professional real estate agents
2. Advance your team of scouts
3. Build a solid wholesaler network
4. Use retailers to buy at discount prices
5. Implement a marketing campaign

Figure 9.1

advantage of. The first of these methods explains the importance of building a qualified network of real estate agents who can serve as your eyes and ears in as many markets as there are agents. We will then discuss the value of building a team of scouts, wholesalers, and retailers who can bring you more deals than you can possibly use. Finally, we will explore the advantages of implementing a marketing campaign that will keep the opportunities flowing. Applying the systems described in this chapter will enable you to launch your real estate investment career at full speed while putting the discovery process of finding undervalued real estate opportunities on autopilot, thereby allowing you to spend more time capitalizing from each of these deals rather than spending time finding them.

Professional and Qualified Real Estate Agents

The first step in placing your acquisition strategy on autopilot is to build a network of professional real estate agents who are qualified to assist you in this process. A common mistake that many beginning investors make is to think that by circumventing the real estate agent, they can save themselves the money that would otherwise have been spent on commissions. While in theory this may make sense, in reality the rationale is fundamentally flawed. Real estate agents should be a vital part of every investor's acquisition team. Real estate agents have thousands of contacts that you do not have. They can serve as your eyes and ears in numerous areas where you cannot be. Don't worry about trying to save a few dollars on a commission. The deals your extensive network of agents can bring you are worth far more than the money saved on one commission.

Although working with real estate agents is important, what is even more important is working with those who actually know what they are doing. Not all real estate agents were created equally. Okay, maybe that's an overstatement, but based on my experience, the range of competency among them varies widely. In *The Complete Guide to Buying and Selling Apartment Buildings* (Hoboken, New Jersey: John Wiley & Sons, 2004), I described two techniques that have the potential to save investors thousands of dollars on each and every real estate transaction. One of these principles is centered on the premise of using real estate agents who are competent in their chosen profession. Ignoring this principle can bring your real estate career to a sudden halt.

The example I used centers on the acquisition and subsequent disposition of an apartment complex I owned and later sold. I had approached a commercial real estate agent about representing me to sell the apartments and asked for his assessment of the property's value. My own analysis of the property's financial statements suggested a value ranging from $2.0 million to $2.1 million. Much to my surprise, after examining the property and its accompanying financial statements, the agent recommended a sales price of $1.8 million on the high side and suggested that I would be fortunate to get even an offer for $1.65 million. Rather than accept the agent's price at face value, I decided to get not only a second opinion, but a third opinion as well. I contacted two other sales agents who were specialists in the apartment industry. Being careful not to prejudice their opinions of the property's worth, I asked them for an estimate of value based on the apartment's financial statements. After reviewing the financial statements, the first agent suggested a value ranging from $2.0 million to $2.1 million, while the second agent suggested a value ranging from $2.0 million to $2.2 million. Their analysis confirmed my own. Needless to say, the first agent did not represent me in this transaction. I sold the property several months later for just under $2.0 million. Had I taken the advice of the first sales agent, it would have cost me $345,000, a sizable sum even by Donald Trump's standards.

The two precepts highlighted in this excerpt are vitally important to your success in the real estate business. The first principle outlined above is one that this entire book is based on. It is that investors must have a complete understanding of the concept of value as it relates to real estate. In the example presented here, not having a working knowledge of this essential real estate precept could have potentially cost me $345,000. The first principle of understanding value is directly related to the second principle, which is what this section is about. Although as the owner I understood the true value of my apartment building, unfortunately the real estate agent I was about to hire did not. The second principle states that the real estate agent or agents you choose to work with must be capable and competent in the real estate industry. It's as simple as that, or so it seems.

Before you take time to develop a solid working relationship with an agent, you should assess his or her level of competency. Many agents are part time and are really not that committed to their work. They're usually just looking to make an extra buck. If they sell a house, great. It they don't, oh well. I suggest you avoid the part-timer and look for someone who loves what they do and has a proven track record of success. You want agents who are in the real estate loop every day and can provide you with fresh opportunities as soon as they hit the market. Your agents should always be on the lookout to present potential deals to you. Before they can do this, however, you must explain your investment criteria to them so they know exactly what you are looking for. Real estate agents work off commissions, so I assure you that when they find an undervalued property they think you may be interested in, they'll let you know. Don't worry about rejecting some of the opportunities they bring to you. Just explain to the agents what you didn't like about it or why it didn't meet your predetermined investment criteria and send them off to find another deal for you. They will respond by bringing you what you are looking for.

While it is important to build and work with a team of competent real estate agents, be careful not to follow them blindly. Take the information they have provided to you and do your own analysis. If you have a difference of opinions, as I did in the apartment example, don't be afraid to take a stand by following your convictions. It may just be that you know something they do not. Of course, the opposite could also be true, but let me share another example with you. I have one agent in particular who brings me deals on a regular basis. This agent deals primarily in real estate owned properties, or REOs, and has over 20 years of experience in several of the neighborhoods in which we buy and sell. Although he has proven to be an excellent source for providing us with undervalued properties, I have noticed that he has the tendency to be much more conservative on the resale values than I am. For example, if he suggests the resale price of a house should be $54,900, I usually add at least another $5,000 or so to that. I believe this discrepancy is a direct result of his personal experience of selling houses in the resale market, which he has a difficult time doing. That's because he's used to working with investor types like me who want the absolute best price on a house. If I take his advice and price the properties where he suggests, it would cost me no less than $5,000 on each and every transaction. So is he a competent real estate agent? Absolutely. Do we have a difference of opinions? Yes. The bottom line, however, is that he knows how to find the kinds of undervalued properties I am looking for. I let him focus on bringing me deals he knows I'll like. I, in turn, focus on getting them sold for top dollar as soon as they're ready to go on the market.

In addition to having a respectable level of competency, using several real estate agents to locate undervalued properties for you rather than using only one or two is one of the best ways to find potential investment opportunities. I recommend developing a relationship with several agents in your area. All people function within their own circles of influence, including real estate agents. While there may be some overlap, no two agents have the same group of friends and business contacts. Using more than one agent will increase your exposure to different opportunities. I'm sure you're familiar with the maxim "two heads are better than one." Smart investors know that when it comes to finding good deals, that saying holds true every time in this business. The more agents in the field looking for undervalued properties for you, the greater your chances of success are. When real estate agents do bring opportunities to you that meet your criteria, be prepared to follow through by purchasing the property. Remember that their time is just as important to them as yours is to you. If they spend a lot of time chasing deals for you and you're not able to execute, there's a good chance they'll drop you like a hot potato. Top agents didn't get where they are by fooling around with buyers who can't perform. I have several agents who are affiliated with different brokerage firms who are constantly on the lookout for undervalued properties for my company. They know that if they find a deal that meets my investment criteria, they've just earned themselves a commission. This is because they know we are very serious about buying undervalued properties and that we have the financial ability to follow through. We don't waste valuable time "thinking about it."

If the deal makes sense, we're on the phone immediately to make an offer to purchase. If you don't already have a network of competent and professional real estate agents on your team, begin today by contacting different offices in your area. The sooner you develop a network of agents, the sooner you'll be able to put your acquisition strategy on autopilot.

Advance Your Team of Scouts

Another method of locating undervalued real estate opportunities the autopilot way is by advancing a team of scouts to go exploring for you. Using scouts is a low-cost and effective way to find undervalued properties because almost anyone can be one. There are no licenses to obtain as there are for real estate agents, and no specialized training is required other than the instructions you give them regarding the types of undervalued investment properties you are seeking, their respective price range, and other general information. You can offer to pay a referral fee, for example, of between $250 and $500 to college students, friends and neighbors, or relatives for every deal they bring you that results in a purchase. The following excerpt, taken from *The Complete Guide to Investing in Rental Properties,* provides some background information on scouts, as well as some of the benefits of using them.

> Scouts who served in the United States Army years ago provided an invaluable service to their captains. They were sent out in advance of the troops to gather information about the enemy's position, their military strength, and possible areas of vulnerability. The scouts would then report back to their captain to disseminate key information about the enemy. Important decisions were then made based on the information gathered by the scout. While military commanders relied heavily on scouts two hundred years ago, they now use a much more advanced type of scout. Today's military leaders rely on sophisticated technology such as radar and satellite imagery to report vital information

such as the enemy's position, how many tanks they have on the ground, and how many troops they have in place. The process itself is much the same though, with important information being provided to those authorized to make decisions. Just as the scouts in the military report vital intelligence to those who have the power to act upon it, so do scouts in a real estate capacity report key information regarding potential investment opportunities to you. A good scout should gather as much information as possible so that you can make prudent decisions.

Scouts can provide important and timesaving information for investors such as:

- The general condition of an investment property
- The location of the property
- An assessment of the neighborhood the property is located in
- The seller's asking price, terms, and timing needs
- The seller's reason for selling and the degree of urgency

A scout's role is similar to that of a real estate agent in that scouts are constantly on the lookout for undervalued investment opportunities that meet your investment criteria. When the scout identifies what he or she believes to be a potential deal, the scout then passes that information along to you to review. Just like real estate agents, scouts are only paid when you actually purchase the property they referred to you. This method of compensation provides scouts with a strong incentive to bring you only the types of properties you are looking for. It also will save you money since you only pay on the basis of performance. Although in some states you may be prohibited from paying a commission to anyone who is not a licensed agent, you can, however, pay that person a referral fee. Like the network of real estate agents, you should begin immediately to build a team of scouts who can augment the research efforts of other members of your team and thereby facilitate the autopilot process.

Build a Solid Wholesaler Network

Another vital step for finding undervalued real estate properties the autopilot way is to build a solid wholesaler network. Similar to the function of a scout, wholesalers play an important role in bringing opportunities to investors by acting as wholesalers for those investors selling at the retail level. Wholesalers, who are often licensed real estate agents, make their money from commissions and, sometimes, a slight markup in the price of the property they are selling. They know that the markup must be minimal so as to leave enough profit in the deal to remain attractive to other investors to whom they will sell. Wholesalers typically have an extensive network of contacts they work with who provide them with inventory to sell. For example, they frequently work with several lenders with whom they have established relationships in order to facilitate the sale of nonperforming assets such as real estate that has been foreclosed on. Because the lenders know the wholesalers will be instrumental in getting these nonperforming assets off their books, they work directly with them in a spirit of cooperation to facilitate these transactions.

Wholesalers who specialize in bank foreclosures act as agents and therefore do not take title to the real estate they sell. There isn't any need to, since their chief function is to represent sellers who desire to dispose of unwanted assets. Buying real estate owned properties directly from banks would create unnecessary transaction costs for the wholesaler. The most efficient way of handling these transactions is for the wholesaler to act as an agent for the lender, thereby allowing the wholesaler to sell directly to investors. Because wholesalers work with several lenders, they typically have several undervalued properties in inventory at any given time. You can get to know those agents in the wholesale market by contacting several real estate companies in your area and asking who is responsible for listing and selling lender real estate owned (REO) properties. Many offices have at least one agent who specializes in lender foreclosures and will be more than happy to work with you.

After all, that's how they make their money. I recommend building a network of several such wholesalers because each of them represents different lenders in different markets. The main disadvantage of purchasing property at the wholesale level is that because they are almost always in need of repair, additional funds will be required to renovate them. Most lenders make loans based on the purchase price of the property, not on the value of it after the improvements have been made. This means a source of funds will be needed to make the necessary renovations. Depending on what your investment objectives are, establishing relationships with wholesalers in different markets will enable you to further accelerate your autopilot program.

Use Retailers to Buy at Discount Prices

The process of retailing involves buying property such as houses below market value, renovating them to like-new condition, and then reselling them at market, or even at a premium to market. Unlike the scout or the wholesaler, the retailer will often take title to the property. Retailers typically hold property anywhere from 30 to 90 days while making improvements to the property, and then offer it for sale to a more permanent type of buyer like a homeowner or investor who will use it for rental purposes. The retailer must have more capital available to work with than a scout or wholesaler because funds are required for the down payment, property improvements, and carrying costs, which include interest payments, taxes, insurance, and utilities, at a minimum. Although the retailer can plan and hope to have a property sold within 30 days after making all the improvements, it may in reality take up to six months to sell, and in some cases even longer. Much like a car dealer who has built up an excess supply of cars in inventory, retailers also can build up excessive inventory. And like the car dealer who sometimes runs a clearance sale to unload some of the excess inventory, so, too, does the retailer who wants to unload some of his or her excess inventory. The carrying costs alone can be enough to restrict the retailer's ability to buy and sell, especially when multiplied by several houses. It's all many people can do to make the payments on one house, let alone 10 or 20 houses. Remember that these houses are non-income-producing as there are no rents being collected. The retailer is in the business of buying and selling, not buying and holding. The retailer's degree of motivation will vary depending on other factors as well, such as how much value was created in previous deals and the timing for entry into the next investment. If, for example, the retailer has identified another opportunity but needs the cash out of this house, then she may be willing to strike a bargain, knowing that she will make up for it, and then some, on the next transaction. Investors who are buying and selling in volume are not interested in holding out for top dollar. They prefer to take a little less and keep their turnover ratio high, knowing that the more houses they buy and sell, the more they will make in the long run.

When the retailer's inventory of houses that are available for sale becomes greater than his ability to comfortably maintain the servicing of related expenses, just like the car dealer, he runs a clearance sale. While it may not be advertised as such, the retailer is no doubt motivated to sell off his excess inventory, especially those houses that have been held in inventory for an extended period of time. If the retailer who has excess inventory doesn't act rapidly, the lack of cash required to cover all the expenses can quickly catch up to him. For that reason, retailers who supposedly sell only at full retail prices sometimes become highly motivated sellers willing to sell at a discount. The cash brought in from a quick sale can enable retailers to service the debt and other related carrying costs on the rest of their inventory, as well as provide additional funds that can be used to invest in more properties.

In addition to offering discounts to unload excess inventory, retailers will oftentimes offer discounts to those customers who do repeat business with them. An investor purchasing rental houses, for example, may prefer to purchase property that has already been cleaned up, renovated, and is available for immediate occupancy by prospective tenants. If the investor knows she can expect a certain level of quality at a fair value from a particular retailer, then it makes sense to her to purchase many, if not all, of her rental houses from the retailer. The retailer, on the other hand, can better control the property's related carrying costs since he knows that as soon as the renovations have been completed and the house is ready for market, he has an investor who is ready to buy it. In addition, the retailer's marketing and advertising costs will be reduced to zero when working with repeat buyers. The savings that result from the reduced carrying and marketing costs can be passed on to the investor, as well as any other price concessions the retailer may be willing to make.

Like wholesalers, retailers are often licensed agents who are affiliated with a local real estate office. Finding retailers to work with is as easy as contacting several of these offices and inquiring who might be in the business of buying, renovating, and selling houses. The main advantages of working with a retailer are that you have a seller you can establish a relationship with who will provide you with properties at discounted prices that have already been renovated. Because all of the improvements have already been made, you don't have to spend your time dealing with contractors. Furthermore, since the costs of the improvements are rolled into the new loan, your out-of-pocket expenses are minimal. The primary disadvantage to purchasing property from a retailer rather than a wholesaler is that you will pay more for it. Working with retailers is nevertheless an excellent way to accelerate your autopilot program as they can provide you with a steady supply of quality properties that meet your specific investment criteria.

Marketing Campaigns

One of the best ways to find undervalued properties is to have sellers bring them to you. The quickest and easiest way to reach them is through one or several of the many advertising mediums that are available to individuals and businesses alike. Recall that in Chapter 3, six traditional methods of finding undervalued properties were listed. The same methods explained there can be used to generate leads from sellers who are motivated and want to sell quickly. Following is a recap of the six methods listed in Chapter 3, along with four additional methods for a total of ten ways to implement an aggressive marketing campaign.

1. Professional associations
2. Classified advertisements
3. Real estate publications
4. Internet Web sites
5. Real estate investment clubs
6. Tax exchange networks
7. Corrugated signs
8. Handouts and flyers
9. Direct mail
10. Business cards

As you join various professional associations and get to know the members, be sure to let them know that you are in the business of buying houses and, more particularly, houses from sellers who are motivated. You also may wish to distribute flyers at events held by professional associations, as well as posting them on bulletin boards as allowed. Another effective yet inexpensive marketing tool used by investors is the classified ad. Your classified ads should be placed in the real estate wanted section of the paper. Don't bother spending a lot of money on these ads. Succinctly written ads can be just as effective as larger and more expensive ads. Your goal is to get people who are motivated and want to sell their houses to call you. The classified ad should be designed to solicit a specific type of call from motivated sellers so that you are not bothered by people who are not likely to have the type of property for sale that you are looking for. Real estate publications are another source for attracting prospective sellers. Place an ad describing the type of property you are looking for, as well as your specific investment criteria. In addition to those individuals selling their own properties, don't be surprised if you have several real estate agents respond to your ad as well. This represents yet another opportunity to interact with professionals who are in the business of representing buyers and sellers every day and who may very well have just the type of property you are looking for at just the right price.

Creating a Web site that describes the types of properties you are interested in is a cost-effective way to provide additional information to motivated sellers. You can direct prospective sellers to your Web site by listing the Web address on your business card, in classified ads, in direct mail pieces, and in practically all other forms of advertising you do. Real estate investment clubs are another place to share information with other investors about the type of property you are looking for. Club members are buyers and sellers too, and they routinely come across deals that may very well fit your specific criteria. You can pass out business cards or distribute flyers at club meetings to make other members aware of the type of property you are looking for. Tax exchange groups represent yet another way of finding undervalued properties the autopilot way. Oftentimes groups such as this, as well as the previously mentioned investment clubs, will share their database of members with other members. In some cases, the lists are sold to nonmembers who may have an interest in doing business with them. I would encourage you not only to procure a copy of the list to do your own direct mail pieces to the members, but also to become a member so that you receive information from other members who may be selling their properties.

Using small, corrugated signs is another great way to attract prospective sellers. Signs are inexpensive and often don't require more than a few days to have made up if you're having custom signs printed. The signs can be placed almost anywhere and can be used to direct sellers to a Web site or to call a telephone number, or both. The signs should contain only a brief message such as "I Buy Houses" along with a phone number and Web address. They should be placed in neighborhoods with which you are familiar and in which you have an interest in investing. Handouts and flyers containing information with the type of investment you are looking for can be used almost anywhere. For instance, flyers can be posted in real estate offices, on bulletin boards available at many businesses, and at the meetings you are already attending as a member of an investment club or professional association. Sending a direct mail piece to the members of the groups with whom you are associated, as well as real estate agents, appraisers, and other real estate professionals is another effective tool for creating an automated system. Finally, one of my favorite ways of gathering names is to ask people I meet for one of their business cards. It doesn't matter if it's the local florist, the neighborhood grocer, or the community banker. I like collecting business cards from anyone and everyone. One of the great things about this practice is that whenever I ask people for their business cards, they almost always will quite naturally ask for one of mine! This gives me the chance to tell them what I do and what types of houses or real estate I am interested in. Rather than throwing the business cards you collect into a drawer and forgetting about them, I recommend that you create a file by entering them into a database for direct mail campaigns. When these recipients open the mail, they can immediately put a face with the name on the flyer or other direct mail piece you sent them.

So there you have it—10 terrific ways to find undervalued properties the autopilot way! You can use any one or all 10 of the methods listed here. The more of these methods you use, the more potential deals will be brought to you, and the more opportunity you will have to find a great, bargain-priced property. Keep in mind that to be successful in this business, you must remain impartial and objective throughout the selection process. Don't fall into the trap of becoming emotionally attached to a property. Doing so will distort your ability to properly analyze its value. You will find yourself embarking down the road of rationalization in an effort to justify your investment decision. Remember to moderate your buying decision with caution, take your time, and, most of all, be patient. You will find just the right undervalued property to fit your specific investment criteria, and probably sooner than you think!

In summary, we examined five methods for finding undervalued properties the autopilot way. Once you take the initial steps required to build your undervalued properties pipeline, you will undoubtedly enjoy a steady flow of opportunities. Whether you are building a network of real estate agents or building a team of scouts, both of these groups can be of tremendous value in finding undervalued properties for you. Investment professionals such as wholesalers and retailers can also be of great value to you in the search for undervalued properties. Finally, be sure to incorporate as many of the 10 marketing suggestions as possible into your autopilot strategy. By applying the systems described in this chapter, you can accelerate your real estate investment goal of finding undervalued real estate opportunities automatically, which will allow you to spend more time profiting from each deal rather than spending time trying to find them.

PART 3

How to Use Options to Purchase Undervalued Properties

10

Fundamentals of Real Estate Options

Introduction to Options

Using options is undoubtedly one of the most powerful ways available to investors today to gain control of real estate. Options give investors the legal right to purchase an asset at a predetermined price within a specified period of time. One of the primary reasons for using options stems from the high degree of leverage that can be obtained when purchasing stocks. Option agreements are used by investors to gain control of an asset without having to take legal title to it, which in turn enables them to avoid expensive transaction costs. Furthermore, options can be exercised quickly, thereby allowing investors to be more efficient with their resources. Options are used by investors every day in the stock market to obtain control of the rights to either buy or sell various types of security instruments, such as stocks and bonds. In addition, an investor has the right to sell her option to other investors any time prior to its expiration. An investor could purchase, for instance, a call option for 500 shares of Dell with an exercise price, or "strike price," of $28. This gives the investor the right to buy shares of Dell at $28 during a period of time set forth within the option agreement. The option period may be, for example, 30 days, 60 days, or even longer. If the price of Dell rises above the strike price of $28 during the option period, the investor can exercise her right to purchase 500 shares at a price of $28 and her position is said to be "in-the-money." She can buy at $28 and hold the shares for an indefinite period of time, or she can take the gain created by the difference in the strike price and the market price by selling the shares immediately after purchasing them. If the price of Dell does not rise above $28 during the stipulated contract period, the investor has the right to simply let the option expire without exercising her right to purchase shares. In this situation, her position is said to be "out-of-the-money." Unless she exercised her right to purchase, the only cost to her would be the price paid for the option. She may, however, sell her option rights to another investor prior to its expiration if she so chooses. The price another investor would be willing to pay is determined in part by the time remaining, or duration, of the contract.

Real estate options work essentially the same way as stock options. Although some sellers may require the buyer to meet additional obligations within the agreement, for instance, assuming responsibility for interest and taxes, these elements of the contract are negotiable. When an option is used for real estate, investors have a contractual right to purchase a specific piece of property at a predetermined price within a given time frame. As with stocks, the option will eventually expire worthless if it is not exercised. At some point before the expiration of the option agreement, the investor may exercise his right to purchase the property at the previously established price. Just as with stocks, since a contractual interest is held in the property, that interest is quite often transferable to another investor. This provision allows the holder of the option agreement to sell the property without ever taking title to it. This is a perfectly legitimate and legal way of selling real estate, and it is done by investors across the nation thousands of times a day. Options are an excellent way for investors to purchase property with very little of their own cash, especially if another buyer is found before having to take title to it. Options also afford investors the opportunity to limit their risk exposure in a specific project to only the premium paid for the option. If the investor decides not to exercise the right to purchase, the option expires worthless and the only thing that is lost is the premium paid for the option.

The Black-Scholes Option-Pricing Model

The Black-Scholes option-pricing model is a mathematical model developed by Fisher Black for the purpose of valuing options. It is the standard by which options are valued today. Time, or t, is one of the variables that help determine the value of an option. In other words, investors have the right to exercise an option at their discretion within a specified period of time. As t becomes progressively shorter, its numerical value becomes smaller and therefore affects the value of an option. For example, the value of an option where t equals 90 days would be greater than the value of an identical option where t equals only 30 days. While it is possible that an investor will buy or sell at precisely the right time to lock in a gain, it is also possible that the option will expire worthless and that the investor will lose the money invested to purchase it. In the case of the investor who purchased a call option for 500 shares of Dell, it is hoped that the price of the stock will rise so that the investor can purchase it at the lower strike price of $28 to take advantage of any gains that might occur as a result of a rise in its price. If the price of Dell stock does not rise above its strike price, there is no benefit to the investor from exercising the option. For instance, if Dell stock is selling at $27.50 on the open market, it would not make sense to exercise the option to purchase the stock at its exercise price of $28. To do so would cost the investor an additional 50 cents per share.

Just as options can be used to gain control of shares of stock, so can options be used to gain control of real estate. Options can be used for any type of property, including undeveloped land, single-family houses, apartment complexes, and commercial buildings. An option agreement grants the right to purchase or sell property to the holder of the option, who may exercise his or her rights at any time prior to its expiration. The use of options can be a powerful tool available to real estate investors who are interested in securing an interest in property without having to take title to it. Options enable investors to gain control of property with very little money down, thereby allowing the use of leverage to be maximized. I recommend, however, that options be used with prudence as time is one of the variables. When t expires, so does the agreement, and any option premium that has been paid will be forfeited at the time of its expiration. Although an unfavorable outcome will result in the loss of any option premium paid, the loss is at least limited to the premium, which can be minimal when compared to the cost of actually purchasing property, taking title to it, and holding it for an extended period of time. Carefully analyze the market as it applies to your particular investment opportunity before committing any capital to it to determine that the probability of the outcome is favorable. If you believe the likelihood for success outweighs the risks assumed within a given option agreement, then assume the risk and execute the agreement. When used properly, options have proven to be a powerful and effective tool for investors to leverage their available assets into incredible wealth-building opportunities.

The Practical Application of Options

Options are a superb tool available to real estate investors that can be used to purchase property with very little cash of their own. In addition, the use of options as an investment tool enables investors to maximize the full power of leverage by gaining control of property with very little money. Another benefit of using options is that they provide investors with the ability to limit their risk exposure in a particular property to only the premium paid for the option. If the investor decides not to exercise the right to purchase, the option expires worthless and all that is lost is the premium paid for the option. Depending on the value of the subject property, an option may potentially cost tens of thousands of dollars. While this may represent a substantial amount of money, keep in mind that the price paid for an option is relative to the value of the property being sought. If, for example, an investor paid $10,000 for an option to buy a $1 million property, the price paid for the option relative to the value of the property is only 1 percent. Using another example, an investor may assess a $2,500 premium for an option to a person who wants to purchase a $50,000 house using a lease option technique to do so. In this example, the premium represents 5 percent of the total purchase price of the property. Although the Black-Scholes model is the standard used to price options for stocks, option premiums for real estate are typically based on whatever price is negotiated by the parties that have an interest in it. Like the Black-Scholes model, however, time is one of the variables taken into consideration by investors when considering the value of an option for real estate. As t increases or decreases, so does the value of the option increase or decrease. In other words, the longer the period of time an investor holds the option for, the greater its value is at the time of purchase. If the investor decided to sell the option at some point in the future, its value would decrease over the time until such point as it expires and becomes worthless.

Now that we have examined the theoretical rationale that drives the price paid for real estate options, let's look at an example of the practical application by using options in a real-life example.

Some of the investment activities used by my company include the use of options for the purchase, development, and eventual construction of houses. Using options enables me to acquire the rights to land without having to take legal title to it until the construction of a new home begins. So, for example, after Symphony Homes enters into a purchase agreement or sales contract with a client to build a new home on one of the optioned lots, we then exercise our option at the predetermined strike price and purchase the lot. The primary benefit of using options in a transaction such as this is that the required option premium as a percentage of the value of the deal is typically less than that required for a purchase using conventional financing. In other words, an investor can often achieve a much higher degree of leverage by using options than by using more conventional financing mechanisms such as bank loans.

On one transaction in particular, I acquired the remaining 28 lots that were appropriate for construction in a residential community through the use of an option agreement. The lots were valued at a little over $1 million, and the option premium in this example was approximately 5 percent, or $50,000. In most cases, I prefer to keep the option premium in the 1 to 2 percent range, but in this particular example, the seller demanded more. In fact, he started out asking for a much higher premium of a little more than $100,000, which I was not at all willing to pay. After negotiating back and forth for several weeks, we finally agreed on 5 percent. Let's now examine the differences between using an option agreement and conventional financing such as that offered by a bank.

Option Agreement:
Purchase Price = $1,000,000
Option Fee = 5%
Total Cash Outlay = $1,000,000 × 5% = $50,000

Conventional Bank Loan:
Purchase Price = $1,000,000
Down Payment = 20%
Total Cash Outlay = $1,000,000 × 20% = $200,000

In this example, you can clearly see the power of added leverage achieved by using an option instead of a conventional bank loan. In this case, I could actually have purchased $4,000,000 worth of property using the $200,000 required for conventional financing as follows.

($200,000/$50,000) × $1,000,000 = $4,000,000 **OR** ($200,000/0.05) = $4,000,000

The advantages of using an option to gain control of the land in this example are twofold. The first advantage is that if our company has difficulty selling new homes to prospective buyers in this particular community, we are not stuck with the ongoing burden and cost of owning the lots. The only thing we have at risk is our option money. While $50,000 is a considerable sum to have exposed to risk, it is much better than having a $200,000 level of exposure. The second advantage is that if we were actually to purchase the lots, the sale would trigger an increase in taxes due to a new and much higher assessed property value since the value of finished lots is much higher than it was when the developer first started improving the land. This is because in the state of Michigan, property values are not reassessed until a transfer of ownership has occurred. Taxes are instead capped at a maximum increase by a change in prices similar to that of the Consumer's Price Index, or CPI. As the new owners, Symphony Homes would then be obligated to assume the new and much higher tax liability.

In summary, the use of options can be an incredibly effective tool available to real estate investors who are interested in gaining control of investment property without having to take title to it. Options afford investors the ability to gain control of property with very little money down, thereby allowing them to maximize the fundamental tool of leverage. In order to avoid the unnecessary loss of an option premium, you must exercise prudence when purchasing options. Recall that time (t) is one of the determinants of value for option agreements. When t expires, so does the option and any premium paid is forfeited unless the option is exercised. Carefully study the market as it applies to your particular investment opportunity before committing any capital to it so as to determine that the probability of the outcome is favorable. This will help minimize the risk of loss of your capital, thereby enabling you to become more successful in your real estate endeavors.

11

High-Leverage Techniques: How to Use Options, Short Sales, and Other Dynamic Strategies for Maximum Gains

In the last chapter, we examined the fundamental precepts by which options function, as well as the many benefits to investors who use them. Two of those benefits deal with an investor's ability to maximize the use of leverage while simultaneously minimizing the level of risk exposure in a given project. In this chapter, we'll explore several high-leverage techniques that have the power to catapult the average individual into a skilled investor who can seemingly create wealth out of thin air. These methods include wealth-building strategies utilizing options, short sales, "subject to" clauses, and hard money (or private money) lenders. First, we'll study two of the more commonly used option strategies employed by investors: purchase options and lease options. Then we'll delve into the world of short sales and discuss the fantastic gains available to investors who implement these techniques. Next, we'll analyze the power of purchasing property "subject to" and look at ways investors can implement this technique. Finally, we'll explore the multitude of possibilities available to investors through hard money and private moneylenders (see Figure 11.1).

Five High-Leverage Techniques for Maximum Gains

1. Purchase options
2. Lease options
3. Art of the short sale
4. Buying "subject to"
5. Private money and hard money loans

Figure 11.1

Purchase Options

Purchase options are used by investors who intend either to take title to real property at a future date or sell it to another buyer prior to taking title. Using purchase options enables investors to gain control of a property without taking title to it initially. As discussed in the previous chapter, options can enable investors to take advantage of real estate opportunities with very little money down, and, in some cases, with no money down. For an option to be legally binding, *valuable consideration* must be given. Although the most common form of consideration given is money, it doesn't have to be. Any consideration that is said to have value is deemed acceptable for the purpose of determining whether or not a contract is considered legally binding. For example, consideration can include the labor for services rendered, an interest in another property or asset, or even love and affection. More specifically, valuable consideration can be labor rendered such as roofing, painting, or general maintenance. It can also be an interest in another asset such as a second mortgage on another rental property, a diamond ring, or a boat or automobile. Finally, valuable consideration can be love and affection given by a spouse, a relative such as a mother-in-law, or even a significant other. In short, valuable consideration can be most anything.

While purchase options grant investors the right to purchase real property for a specific price any time prior to their expiration, they are also oftentimes assignable. This means that an investor who has an option on a small apartment complex, for example, can sell the rights granted to her within the agreement to another investor. In other words, the rights and provisions contained within the option agreement can be assigned, or sold, to another investor who will then have the same right to purchase as the original investor. This allows the investor to transfer her interest in the property for a profit or other valuable consideration without ever taking title to it. Because this can be done with the mere stroke of a pen in a matter of minutes, transaction costs are greatly reduced for both parties. If the new buyer of the option decides to exercise his right to purchase by actually taking title to the property, depending on the type of financing mechanism used, transaction costs will likely increase to a more normal level. Let's look at an example. Investor A wants to sell his 20-unit apartment building for $500,000. Investor A grants Investor B an option to purchase the building at any time during the next six months for 1 percent, or $5,000. It is also agreed that the option premium will be applied toward the purchase price if Investor B exercises her rights within the stipulated time period. Investor B then contacts Investor C, who she knows is looking for an apartment building in this price range. Investor B negotiates a sales price of $525,000 with Investor C. At the closing, title passes directly from Investor A to Investor C. Investor A receives the remaining balance of $495,000 less closing costs. Meanwhile, Investor B receives $25,000 for her efforts in putting the deal together plus the return of her original option fee. Although it is true that the $5,000 option premium she paid was at risk, because she knew the market well, she was very comfortable with assuming the risk. As previously described, options are powerful tools available to investors, but prudence and confidence must be exercised in the particular market in which they are being used.

Another purchase option technique for investors not wanting to take title to a property eliminates the assignment step. For example, if you used a purchase option to gain control of an undervalued single-family house and then found another buyer for the house before the option expired, the new buyer of the house would take title directly from the persons or parties who granted you the option, but at the price and terms you have negotiated with them. Once again, this technique is very useful in gaining control of real property without having to finance the property, without having to take title to it, and without having to incur expensive transaction costs. In the example above, Investor B could have assigned her rights to Investor C for $10,000 or any other amount the two of them had agreed upon.

The following story is an experience I shared in *The Complete Guide to Flipping Properties* (Hoboken, New Jersey: John Wiley and Sons, 2003). In this particular example, I used a purchase option strategy to gain control of 28 vacant lots in a community that was partially built out with new homes, but that had been abandoned by the previous builder who had apparently suffered a financial setback. The story not only serves to illustrate the power of the purchase option strategy, but also serves to illustrate the kind of value that can be unlocked from a distressed property that is purchased from a distressed builder by making a combination of simple and cost-effective improvements. In this example, the combination of improvements included a simple cleanup of the property, as well as general landscaping improvements. Keep these wealth-building strategies in mind as you read the following excerpt.

As an investor who is serious about flipping properties, you *must* be able to look beyond what you see on the surface. While most people see a lump of coal, you will come to recognize it as a diamond that just needs a little polishing. Ideally, you will be able to buy houses and sell them at diamondlike prices.

As a principal for Symphony Homes, I recently took over an entire community that was partially completed with new homes and successfully applied the value play strategy. The community was only about three years old, but the original builder there apparently ran into financial difficulty, which caused the progress of new home construction to come to a standstill. As a result, the entrance way and all of the remaining vacant lots became neglected. Weeds and grass went uncut and grew as high as four to five feet. Many of the vacant lots were littered with debris left over from the previous builder. In short, the community was a real eyesore! The developer of the subdivision had tried unsuccessfully for over six months to get another builder to come in and take over where the previous builder had left off. No one would touch it. Discussions with the city inspectors led me to believe that even they had written the community off.

As it turned out, our company was able to negotiate a very favorable price and subsequently took over the remaining lots. As a condition for doing so, the developer agreed at his expense to have all of the vacant lots mowed, the debris removed, and the entrance way cleaned up immediately upon closing. Within one week, the community was cleaned up and a sense of pride was restored to the residents who lived there.

Although purchasing the property in this example had several drawbacks, there were other factors that could be taken into consideration to compensate for them. For example, while the entrance to the community was unsightly and overgrown with weeds, landscaping improvements would be quick and inexpensive to make. Additionally, although most of the vacant lots were overgrown with weeds and littered with debris, the weeds could easily be cut and the debris picked up. Finally, while the residents and the city had all but given up hope for the community, I believed that because the existing homes in it were only three years old and it was in an ideal location, the minor improvements such as mowing and cleanup, along with an effective marketing campaign, would be enough to get the community back on the right track.

As you can see by this example, the purchase option technique can be used to gain control of not only single-family houses, but in this case, an entire community of vacant lots. Using the purchase option technique gave me the right to buy the remaining lots over an extended period of time with much less of my own capital than otherwise would have been required using a more conventional financing source such as a bank. With a minimum amount of capital, I was able to maximize the company's leverage while simultaneously minimizing its risk. This technique can be used with most any type of real estate including single-family houses, multifamily apartment complexes, commercial buildings, vacant land, office buildings, and even industrial sites. The purchase option technique is a powerful way to leverage a variety of real estate opportunities and is limited only by your imagination.

Lease Options

A lease option is similar to a purchase option in that it grants investors the right to purchase property at a predetermined price within a stipulated period of time. Lease options combine the basic lease or rental agreement with an option to purchase contract. The primary difference between these methods, however, is that lease options are typically used with property such as a single-family dwelling that might otherwise be rented to a tenant. For example, if you sell a house using the lease option technique, your buyer/tenant is granted the right to purchase it within a specified period of time for an agreed upon price. As a purchaser of property using this technique, you may be given control of a rental house and have the right to sublease the property if so desired, provided the owner of the property has granted this right within the agreement. This type of provision allows investors to control property without actually purchasing it, lease it out, and look for a buyer—all with a minimum amount of money. Under the lease option agreement, a nonrefundable option fee, or some other form of valuable consideration, is given instead of a rental deposit, which is typically refundable. Furthermore, a portion of the monthly lease amount is typically applied toward the purchase price. This is, in effect, similar to getting a loan or mortgage on a house in that a portion of the payment is applied toward reducing the principal loan balance each month. At a time specified within the lease option agreement, the buyer can exercise her right to purchase the property and pay off the remaining loan balance with a new loan if desired. If at some time during the option period the purchaser finds another buyer, then she may exercise her right without ever taking legal title to the property by creating a sale that transfers legal interest in the property directly from the original seller to the buyer who is purchasing from the lessee. If, on the other hand, the lessee decides not to exercise her right to purchase, control reverts back to the original owner who is then entitled to keep the option money deposit as well as any portion of the monthly lease payments that would have been applied toward the purchase price.

In general, the lease option technique is one of the quickest and least expensive methods available to investors for buying and selling real property. There are several advantages to using the lease option technique. One of the primary advantages is that the purchaser is not required to conform to the various underwriting guidelines that banks and other lenders require. In addition, buyers can often option a property with very little down, which in turn enables them to increase their buying power. The seller, unlike an underwriter working for a mortgage company, is likely to require very little in the way of documentation. The seller providing the financing doesn't really care where the money for the down payment comes from just as long as it comes from some-where. To the seller, cash is cash whether it comes from an advance on a MasterCard or Visa, from a home equity line of credit (HELOC) loan, or from a personal savings account. The more traditional lenders like banks and mortgage companies, on the other hand, can be very partic-ular where the money for a down payment comes from. In many cases, the money cannot even come from a family member or friend. Moreover, with this type of stipulation, borrowers must be able to prove that the money is their own and did not come from a relative. Another advantage of using the lease option technique is that it allows investors to save money by avoiding the fees and transaction costs commonly charged for new loans. For example, there are no loan application fees, no underwriting fees, no loan origination fees, no real estate commis-sions, and no points to be paid. Remember also that the option fee is nonrefundable, unlike most rental deposits. Finally, the time needed to close on a transaction when using a lease option is much less than for traditional financing arrangements since there is no loan approval process, appraisal, survey, or title search required.

One caveat to be aware of when using the lease option technique is the due-on-sale provision embodied within almost all mortgage instru-ments. This clause gives the lender, or mortgagee, the right to acceler-ate the loan balance in the event that the borrower, or mortgagor, sells or transfers his or her right in the property. The due-on-sale provision, however, applies more to individuals who sell their property outright such as with a land contract or owner financing arrangement. With a lease option, the seller's interest in the property is not transferred until such time as the buyer exercises his right to purchase the property. At that time, conventional financing is often used to replace any existing debt on the property. The due-on-sale contract is a contractual right and not a law, so don't be intimidated by tough-sounding language. Lenders first began using due-on-sale provisions in the 1980s, when interest rates rose dramatically, to prevent buyers from assuming an existing loan rather than taking out a new loan since the interest rates on existing loans were lower. The banks used the due-on-sale provision to attempt to force homeowners to borrow at the newer and higher rates. Homeowners fought back by claiming that enforcement of the due-on-sale provision was an unfair trade practice. Although the homeowners won this initial battle, lenders lobbied Congress to pass a federal law that would supersede the courts. The lenders ultimately won and the Garn-St. Germaine Federal Depository Institutions Act was passed. The Garn law gives lenders the right to enforce the due-on-sale provision, but it also includes a few exceptions in which the lender may not enforce it, such as allowing a homeowner to transfer title to a living trust for his or her own benefit. In general, the only time a due-on-sale provision is likely to be enforced is if the payments are delinquent. If that were the case, the lender would then most likely foreclose on the loan rather than enforce the due-on-sale provision.

When using the lease option technique as a seller, you should try to collect the maximum amount of option money you can. The more buyers or tenants have invested into your property, the better they will take care of it and the more likely they will be to exercise their option when the time comes. The amount of the premium will vary depending on where your property is located. In general, an option premium for an average-priced single-family house can range anywhere from $1,000 to $5,000, and sometimes more. An average-priced house in one area, however, may be $100,000 while in other areas it may be $250,000 or more. I suggest charging whatever the market will bear in your particular area. If you start out asking for a nonrefundable premium of $10,000 and meet some resistance by the buyers or tenants, ask them what amount they would be comfortable with. So long as the amount they respond with meets your minimum requirements, then you can proceed with the agreement. Remind the buyers that since they intend to purchase the house anyway, whatever amount they pay for the option will be used to reduce the purchase price of the house. The amount charged for the monthly payment should at a minimum cover all of the monthly obligations for the property. If you want to demonstrate an attitude of cooperation and willingness to work with the buyers, you also can give them a credit for a small portion of the amount paid each month to be applied toward the purchase price of the house. This allows them to "build equity" in the house even though they are really only leasing it.

Let's look at an example to see how the monthly rent credit works. Suppose you have a buyer who has signed a lease option agreement for a single-family house that gives him the right to purchase it at any time during the next 12-month period. If you gave the buyer $100 per month in credit toward the purchase of the house, at the end of the 12-month option period, the buyer would have accrued a total of $1,200 in credits that could be applied toward the purchase price or even toward the closing costs. If you wanted to be a little more generous and offer the buyer $200 per month in credits, for example, you could simply increase the price of the house by the corresponding amount, which in this case would be an additional $1,200 ($100 increase times 12 months = $1,200).

In short, the lease option technique is similar to a purchase option in that it grants the right to investors to purchase property at a predetermined price within a stipulated period of time. The lease option technique, however, combines the basic lease or rental agreement with an option to purchase contract. Whether you are a buyer or a seller, lease options provide greater flexibility in structuring transactions while simultaneously reducing your level of risk.

The Art of the Short Sale

In Chapter 6, we discussed several ways to purchase undervalued properties that are in any one of the four phases of foreclosure. While there are numerous techniques that can be used to make money buying and selling foreclosed properties, one of the biggest challenges investors face is finding deals that have enough equity in them to be worth pursuing. For example, if a house appraises for a market value of $250,000, but has a first mortgage in the amount of $200,000 and a second mortgage in the amount of $50,000, there is no equity left in it to make any money. In fact, an investor purchasing the house in this example would most likely lose money by the time all of the transaction costs are factored in. The average investor typically walks away from these types of deals because they mistakenly believe there is no opportunity to profit. The more sophisticated investor, however, recognizes that with a little additional effort, the opportunity to make huge profits is just a few phone calls away. That's where understanding the art of the *short sale* can have a significant impact on an investor's ability to profit from property that is in foreclosure. If the term *short sale* is new to you, it is best understood as getting a lender to accept less than what is owed on a mortgage note. In other words, by successfully negotiating with specialists in the lender's loss mitigation department, investors can quite often convince them to discount the mortgage note. You are most likely already familiar with or have seen private investors who offer to buy notes at a discount. Their advertisements can be found in most real estate publications or classified sections of larger metropolitan newspapers and typically read something like "I BUY NOTES." Investors specializing in the purchase of notes seldom buy them at 100 percent of face value. Notes are commonly discounted as a percentage of face value.

Let's look at an example. Several years ago I sold a mobile home to a young couple for $17,500. The couple agreed to a down payment of $2,500, leaving a loan balance of $15,000, which I agreed to owner finance at an interest rate of 12 percent amortized over a 10-year period. After one year of receiving payments from the couple, I decided to sell the note to an investor. The loan balance at the end of the first year was $14,173. The investor offered me $11,338, or 80 percent of the face value of the note. This represents a difference of $2,835 between the face value of the note and the amount I was offered for it. Your first reaction might be, "Who in their right mind would accept less than the full amount of a note?" The answer is many people. In fact, there are entire industries developed around this concept. Large retailers and manufacturers sell their receivables every day at a discount to raise cash for working capital. This process is referred to as *factoring* and is no different than the investor's buying notes at a discount from guys like me trying to raise cash for the next deal. This brings us back to the concept of the short sale. Lenders will gladly accept a discount on notes that have been foreclosed on because it often makes sound financial sense to do so. In the case of a first mortgage for, let's say, $100,000, lenders will consider accepting as little as 60 to 70 percent of the full value for the simple reason that doing so will mitigate impending losses that are likely to occur if they try to dispose of the property through conventional means on the open market. First of all, the condition of the property will most likely have deteriorated, and the longer it sits vacant, the more the deterioration will continue. Second, the costs of retaining the property in the lender's portfolio can quickly add up. These costs include lost interest on the note for money that could be loaned elsewhere, property taxes, utilities, maintenance and upkeep, legal fees, and the list goes on and on. Furthermore, property that has been foreclosed on shows up on the lender's balance sheet as a nonperforming asset. If the ratio of nonperforming assets approaches or exceeds the allowable limits, the lender will be placed on the federal regulator's watch list and at some point action may be taken against him or her. The bottom line is that lenders are very motivated to move these bad loans off their books as quickly as possible and are therefore motivated to accept short sale offers from investors like you.

The process of short selling requires you to act as an intermediary between the owner of the house in foreclosure and the lender. In order to be successful in this process, there are several steps to consider when short selling mortgages. First of all, you must have a good relationship with the homeowner so that you may represent him or her.

Remember that during this period, the homeowner, not the lender, is still the legal owner of the property, so you must work through the homeowner and obtain his permission to contact the lender and negotiate in his behalf. Let's look at an example. Say a homeowner in distress responds to one of the many marketing methods you are using and states that she is in foreclosure. She says the house is worth about $140,000, that the loan balance is around $136,000, and that she is six months behind on her payments. She also states that the house has been listed for sale for several months with a local real estate agent for $148,000 just to break even after paying all of the related closing costs. Because the house is priced above other houses in her neighborhood, she has had a difficult time selling it. In order for you to profit from a deal like this, the lender must be willing to accept a short sale. The first step then is to meet with the homeowner and have her sign an Authorization to Release information form. This form gives the bank permission to speak with you about the account and eventually to begin the negotiation process. Although not widely publicized, most banks or lenders will have a department that is responsible for non-performing assets typically referred to as the "loss mitigation department." The name of the department is certainly fitting, since that is precisely what the lenders are attempting to do—mitigate their losses. They do this through a variety of methods, one of which is negotiating with investors through the short sale process. Once you have contacted the person responsible for the seller you are working with, explain to him or her that you are attempting to purchase the home from the seller, but that she owes more than it is worth, especially since it is in such poor condition. Explain also that as an investor you will incur repair costs, carrying costs, and transaction costs and that in order to make a reasonable profit, you can only afford to pay $85,000 for the house. Support the value of your offer with a detailed list of repairs, photos, and sales comps for the neighborhood. Explain to the person handling the account that you would like very much to work with him or her in helping to get this property off the books as a nonperforming asset, but that in order to do so, you must be able to buy it at the right price. The lender will then review all of the information you have presented and make a decision based in part on what you have submitted, but also on his or her own internal criteria. Assume the lender responds to your offer with a counteroffer of $110,000. You politely but firmly remind him or her that you are an investor and that if you have to pay that much for the house in addition to all of the repairs and transaction costs, the numbers don't work for you and that you'll have to take a pass. You then suggest that, while you would prefer to purchase the house at the originally offered price of $85,000, you think you can make it work at $95,000, but that is your final offer. Because this particular lender is reasonable and is willing to accept the loss just to move the loan out of the nonperforming assets, your offer is accepted. The next step is to obtain a new loan, then pay off the old loan and pay the seller whatever amount you agreed on, and the house is yours. The amount you agree to give the seller is generally minimal and just enough to help her move out and maybe cover the first month's rent at the place she is moving to. You could certainly give her more, but keep in mind that you just did the seller a big favor by keeping her credit from being ruined for the next several years. Furthermore, although you had nothing to do with getting her into this mess, you had everything to do with getting her out of it. The seller should be thanking you for at least allowing her to get out of the house without being foreclosed on.

In summary, mastering the art of the short sale can be a powerful and effective way to turn a deal with no equity in it that looks hopeless into a lucrative transaction. The process requires a little bit of your time, the patience and skill to act as an intermediary between the homeowner and the lender, and the skills to negotiate a deal that makes sense for all of you. Remember also that when the short sale technique is used, not only are you helping yourself become a successful real estate investor, but you are also helping a distressed homeowner by offering the chance to start over with his or her credit intact.

Buying "Subject To"

Using the "subject to" technique is another powerful and effective way to purchase real estate with little or no money down. The term is used to refer to buying property *subject to* an existing mortgage and is similar to assuming a loan, but with several very important differences. The assumption of a mortgage is an obligation undertaken by the purchaser to be personally liable for payment of an existing mortgage. In an assumption, the purchaser is substituted for the original mortgagor, or borrower, in the mortgage instrument, and the original mortgagor is then released from further liability in the assumption. The purchaser then becomes responsible for all of the terms and conditions set forth in the mortgage and related promissory note. The mortgagee's, or lender's, consent is usually required for a loan assumption. The original mortgagor should always obtain a written release from further liability if he or she desires to be fully released under the assumption. Failure to obtain such a release renders the original mortgagor liable if the person assuming the mortgage fails to make the monthly payments. The assumption of loans was a common method of buying houses in the decades prior to the 1980s. It was used to reduce the costs of obtaining a new loan and to facilitate the purchase process in general. After interest rates began rising sharply in the early 1980s, however, lenders began using the due-on-sale provisions previously discussed in the section on lease options to force buyers to borrow at the new, higher rates. Although most loans today are not assumable, responsibility for them can be transferred using the subject to technique. An assumption of a mortgage is sometimes confused with purchasing subject to a mortgage. When a buyer purchases subject to a mortgage, the buyer agrees to make the monthly mortgage payments on the existing mortgage, but the original borrower remains personally liable if the buyer fails to make the monthly payments. Since the original borrower remains liable in the event of default, the lender's consent is *not* required for a sale subject to a mortgage. While both methods, the assumption of a mortgage and purchasing subject to a mortgage, are used to finance the sale of property, purchasing subject to is more widely used since the lender's consent is not required.

The subject to method is especially effective when negotiating with a seller who is in financial distress and desires to sell the property to avoid foreclosure. The property can quickly and easily be transferred out of the seller's name and into yours by using a *quitclaim deed*. A quitclaim deed is a deed used to transfer whatever interest the maker of the deed may have in a particular property. A quitclaim deed is often given to clear the title when the grantor's interest in a property is questionable, such as a seller who is in financial distress. By accepting such a deed the buyer assumes all the risks since no warranty is given as with a standard deed. Such a deed makes no warranties as to the title, but simply transfers to the buyer whatever interest the grantor, or seller, has. Although the risk is in a technical sense transferred to the buyer, the original promissory note and mortgage instrument are still in the name of the seller; therefore, it is the seller who is truly at risk. You also can have a title search run prior to transferring the property into your name to determine if there are any more outstanding liens or judgments against the property. This preliminary title report will provide you with the information necessary to make an informed decision about whether or not to proceed with the transfer. Purchasing a house subject to the existing mortgage gives the buyer control of the property, but leaves full liability with the seller. A seller in financial distress, such as one who is about to lose her house to the bank in a foreclosure proceeding, will gladly consider the subject to option because it affords her the ability to salvage her credit.

Let's look at an example. Assume a seller who is in default on his mortgage responds to one of your direct mail pieces and wants to sell his house. The seller estimates his house is worth about $100,000, has a remaining loan balance on his mortgage of $40,000, and is three months behind on his payments. He has recently received letters from the bank threatening legal action and foreclosure if he doesn't bring the loan current immediately. The seller, who recently went through a divorce, also just lost his job. At this stage in his life, he really doesn't care about the house any more, but he would like to do whatever he can to protect his credit, knowing that he will need it to rebuild his life at some point in the future. This scenario represents an ideal situation for you to introduce the seller to the subject to technique. Explain to the seller that you can relieve him of his financial obligations immediately, thereby allowing him to move on with rebuilding his life. I suggest starting with an offer just high enough to cover the back payments and provide the seller with a little bit of cash to move out. In this example, you would agree to assume responsibility from the seller to pay his monthly obligation to the lender, make up the three months in back payments, and give him $2,500 for moving and renting expenses. After he accepts the offer, put the agreement in writing using a standard purchase agreement or sales contract, but with a provision in it that states that you are purchasing the property subject to the seller's existing mortgage. After confirming that there are no other liens or judgments against the property, the seller then assigns his rights in the property to you via a quitclaim deed. You have just gained control of a $100,000 asset in which you have an immediate $60,000 in equity (less your costs to buy the seller out) and all you have at risk is the money spent to cash the seller out! If, for whatever reason, you fail to make the required payments, the lender will pursue the individual whose name is on the mortgage, which is the person who sold it to you—the seller. Of course, you have no intention of allowing that to happen. After all, the reason you bought it to begin with was either to turn it for a quick profit or add it to your portfolio of income-producing properties and rent it out. With only a $40,000 loan balance, the property should easily have a positive cash flow. Rather than renting the property out, an alternative is to lease option the property. This would enable you to recoup the initial cash outlay required when you purchased the property. Another option in this situation is to keep the property as a rental (or lease option), but refinance it to raise cash. Because many lenders will gladly loan 80 to 90 percent of value on investment property, you could easily put $40,000 to $50,000 in your pocket. Doing so would then transfer the original seller's mortgage obligations to you because you would be responsible for signing the new mortgage documents—not the seller. This process also would necessitate performing a full title search as the new lender will require a title mortgage insurance policy. Although the policy is meant to insure the lender's interest in the property, it also protects you, the borrower, since any hidden encumbrances would be revealed. The subject to technique, however, was effective in allowing you to gain control of the property while exploring the various options available to you.

Buying subject to can potentially cause some concerns for the seller. For example, the seller will want to be assured that, once you assume responsibility for the loan payments, they are being paid on time each month. This concern can be addressed in one of two ways. The first way is to assure the seller that you are a professional real estate investor, that you keep very good records, and that you will be happy to mail him a copy of the lender's loan statement, which shows the payment history, as it is received each month. An alternative is to use a loan servicing company, which can both collect funds and disperse them. For example, if you rented the property out or sold it on a lease option, the loan servicing company could collect the payments from the new tenant or buyer and subsequently disperse the required funds to the lender. The loan servicing company can generate monthly and annual reports and mail them to the seller as evidence that the payments have been made. The annual report is especially important for the new buyer under a lease option agreement since it contains payment history records that will be useful for obtaining a new loan when the option expires. The buyer must be able to demonstrate to the lender that not only is he current on the payments, but also that they have been made on time over the previous year. Having a third-party service involved that will make the payments as instructed should be sufficient to alleviate the seller's concerns about the payments being made in a timely fashion. Another concern the seller may have is that when she goes to get a new loan on another house, the existing loan on the property sold under a subject to agreement still shows up on her credit report. This concern can be addressed by explaining to the seller that, first of all, since she is just coming out of a state of foreclosure, it is unlikely that she will be applying for a new loan any time soon. When she does get her financial life in order, however, she can present the new lender with a copy of the purchase agreement showing that the property has been sold. In addition, when the lender pulls her credit report, the payments will show up as being current, which will benefit her since the payments have been made on time. The timely payment history should furthermore have a positive effect on her credit score and actually pull it up. At a minimum, the lender should give her credit for 75 to 80 percent of the payment amount, which is similar to an investor owning rental property.

In summary, using the subject to technique can be a dynamic force that provides both you and the seller with several key benefits. The subject to method of purchasing property is quick and efficient, reduces transaction costs, allows the property to be easily transferred with a quitclaim deed, and enables the seller's credit to be salvaged. Moreover, using this method will enable you to take maximum advantage of the power of leverage by purchasing real estate with very little down and, in some cases, by making a few back-payments for the seller. By using the subject to method to purchase undervalued properties from sellers who are in distress, you can amass a real estate portfolio that even Warren Buffett would be proud of!

Private Money and Hard Money Loans

For all practical purposes, the two phrases *private money loan* and *hard money loan* are synonymous with each other and are often used interchangeably. The terms are used to refer to loans that originate from either private investors acting individually, or those who are working collectively through a lending network such as a mortgage brokerage firm. Although private money sources are not well known in the more traditional financing arena, they are well known to many investors who specialize in short-term rehab projects. The typical private money borrower is a solid individual or business that has an opportunity that does not fit well into a conventional and more rigid structure of institutional lending such as that found at a bank. Private money borrowers also desire speed and flexibility unavailable through more conventional means. The term *private money loan* stems from the fact that these loans typically originate from private lending sources as opposed to larger public lenders such as conventional banks and mortgage companies. The term *hard money loan* refers to the financing terms that are said to be hard (or high) for these loans. In short, the fundamental idea of private money lending is that private individuals who have excess funds to invest choose to lend those funds, usually on real estate secured transactions, with the desire to receive a fair rate of return on their investment that is commensurate with the level of risk for the money being loaned. Larger private investors are typically incorporated and use lines of credit as a source for the funds that they lend. In other words, they borrow at a rate that is lower than what they can lend the money out for. The difference between the two rates is referred to as the *spread* and represents the investor's profit on the money lent.

Perhaps more important as a defining characteristic of private money is the process and criteria by which the money is allocated to loans. Private money is quite different from institutional money in several ways. First, with private moneylenders, there is generally greater flexibility with regard to the types of loans and circumstances under which money will be lent. Private moneylenders know their borrowers are most often looking for short-term financing that does not fit into any one of the more traditional loan types offered by banks. Additionally, the strength of the collateral is usually more important to private moneylenders than the qualifications of the borrower. Private moneylenders want assurance that their loans are secure, so the loan-to-value ratios may only range from 50 to 75 percent of the completed value. This means that you can actually get up to 100 percent of the loan amount needed. For example, if you bought a house for $50,000 that needed $20,000 in repairs and would be worth $100,000 when finished, a private moneylender loaning at a 50 percent LTV ratio would actually provide 100 percent of the acquisition cost ($100,000 × 50% = $50,000). Some private moneylenders will also provide funding for the repairs. In this example, the additional $20,000 needed for repairs would increase the total LTV ratio to 70 percent of the completed value. The lower LTV ratios associated with these types of rehab loans provide private money-lenders with the security they need to invest their private capital. If the borrower defaults, the lender is protected and should be able to recoup his or her investment at a minimum. While specific loan programs vary from lender to lender, many of them frequently provide up to 100 per-cent of the acquisition cost, as well as related closing costs, providing that the loan amounts fall within their preestablished parameters. This enables investors to purchase rehab projects with no money down using 100 percent financing from the lender. Receiving the funds needed for repairs varies from lender to lender also, but oftentimes these funds are also available at 100 percent, especially if you have a good track record as an investor who can buy and sell successfully. The money set aside for repairs is generally lent once the repairs have been completed and an inspection has been made, so if you don't have the money to pay the sub-contractors as soon as they've completed their work, you'll need to make arrangements with them to agree to getting paid when the funds from the loan are disbursed.

Another important distinction between private money loans and conventional loans is that private money loans tend to be more expen-sive. For example, using today's interest rates of prime plus one or prime plus two would place the rate of interest being charged at 5 to 6 percent. This compares to an interest rate ranging from 12 to 18 percent, and sometimes more, for private money loans. Furthermore, while zero points or perhaps one point may be paid to originate a conventional loan, four to eight points is not uncommon for a private money loan. Although these rates are high when compared to conventional loans, remember that private money loans are to be used when conventional financing is not available. If you were given a choice, for example, between making $20,000 on a rehab project and paying five points for the loan, or not making $20,000 and paying zero points for the loan you couldn't get, my guess is that you would opt to pay the points and take the $20,000. No one likes to pay a high rate of interest for a loan or cough up a lot of money for points, but if it means the difference between making a deal and not making a deal, I suggest you take what you can get. After all, half of a pie is better than no pie at all.

Finally, private money loans differ from conventional loans in that they are generally easier to get approved. Although private moneylenders do look at the strength and creditworthiness of the borrower, they also place considerable emphasis on the strength of the project itself. So while some experience is preferred, it isn't always necessary to obtain a loan. As far as the investor's credit is concerned, more often than not, private moneylenders will consider borrowers with less than perfect credit. Lenders look for borrowers who have established a pattern of repaying loans on time, realizing that many of them may have hit a few bumps in the road along the way. A red flag for private moneylenders, however, is a pattern of blatant disregard for debt obligations over an extended period of time. It's one thing, for example, for an individual to get laid off from a job for three or four months and fall behind on her payments. It's quite another thing, however, to consistently pay late over several years and, in some cases, not to pay at all. The bottom line with most private moneylenders is that if you can demonstrate to them that you can make the scheduled payments on time, there's a pretty good chance that you'll be able to qualify for a loan. As far as the financial strength of the borrower goes, the primary concern is to determine that the borrower has enough income, or enough cash, or enough liquid assets to complete the project. That means the borrower must have the ability to make the scheduled payments over the life of the project, as well as be prepared for unforeseen problems that may arise, such as cost overruns. Private moneylenders recognize that their customers are in the process of building wealth and oftentimes start with almost nothing. Private moneylenders fill the void left by conventional lenders who are required to adhere to much more stringent federal standards, thereby enabling many investors to take advantage of opportunities that they may not otherwise be able to take advantage of. Figure 11.2 shows a partial list of some of the documents private moneylenders may require.

Loan Documentation Checklist

- ☐ Lender's loan application forms
- ☐ Copy of executed agreements between buyer and seller, including the purchase agreement and related addenda
- ☐ Financial statement showing personal assets as well as additional real estate owned
- ☐ Income and balance statements for your business, if applicable
- ☐ Income tax returns for a minimum of the previous two years—both personal and business
- ☐ Verification of cash required for down payment and reserves: bank statements, savings and retirement account information, other applicable assets
- ☐ Credit references along with full FICO reports
- ☐ Analysis of rehab project with complete estimate of repairs
- ☐ Comparable sales data for recently sold houses in area
- ☐ Projected sales price of subject property and profit
- ☐ Leases used for the subject property as applicable
- ☐ Verification of property taxes for the subject property
- ☐ Insurance binder for rental property
- ☐ Third-party reports, including property survey and appraisal

Figure 11.2

Take a minute to study Table 11.1, Property Analysis Worksheet for Wood Lane. The worksheet you see is a proprietary model I developed that I use to quickly and easily analyze potential rehab investment opportunities for undervalued properties. I call it *The Value Play Rehab Analyzer*. Once I have gathered the necessary data, I can input the information into the model and in less than five minutes know within a reasonable degree of accuracy whether or not a deal makes sense, based on my investment criteria. All I have to do is key in the information and the model automatically makes all of the calculations. For this example, I have not included all the explanatory notes on precisely how the model works because this is not a book on rehabbing or financial analysis. The worksheet was included to illustrate the type of analysis that a private moneylender may ask for. The Rehab Analyzer shows the purchase price, estimate of repairs, comparable sales, estimated selling price, and expected profit for the subject property all in one neat and concise model. For those readers who may be interested, detailed explanations and illustrations of the Rehab Analyzer and other financial models are available in *The Complete Guide to Real Estate Finance for Investment Properties: How to Analyze Any Single-Family, Multifamily, or Commercial Property* (Hoboken, New Jersey: John Wiley & Sons, 2004), as well as in *The Complete Guide to Flipping Properties*, mentioned earlier. For more information on the Rehab Analyzer, see Afterword.

In summary, we've examined several high-leverage techniques that have the power to help propel your ability as an investor into stratospheric heights, thereby enabling you to accelerate your investment goals. Whether you use purchase options or lease options, short sales, subject to clauses, or private moneylenders, each of these wealth-building strategies can enable you to maximize leverage opportunities while simultaneously minimizing your level of risk exposure.

The use of purchase options can enable investors to quickly gain control of real estate without having to take title to it and put very little money down, in some cases, with no money down. Lease options add

Table 11.1 Property Analysis Worksheet for Wood Lane

Purchase Assumptions		Financing Assumptions – Primary			Financing Assumptions – Secondary		
Project Name: Rehab		Primary Mortgage or Loan:			Secondary Financing/Line of Credit:		
Address: 2013 Wood Ln		Total Purchase	100.00%	22,950	Total Imprvmnts	100.00%	12,781
City, State, Zip: Flint, MI 48503		Down Payment	10.00%	2,295	Down Payment	10.00%	1,278
Contact: Steve Berges		Balance to Finc	90.00%	20,655	Balance to Finc	90.00%	11,503
Telephone: (810) 658-3600							
			Annual	Monthly		Annual	Monthly
Land	0	Interest Rate	6.000%	0.500%	Interest Rate	7.500%	0.625%
Building/House	22,200	Amort Period	30	360	Amort Period	30	360
Closing Costs	750	Payment	1,486	124	Payment	965	80
Other Related Costs	0	Interest Only	1,239	103	Interest Only	863	72
Total Purchase Price	22,950						

Estimate for Improvements						
Appliances		Flooring		Lighting		250
Dishwasher	0	Carpet	1,148	Masonry		0
Disposal	0	Ceramic Tile	0	Other		0
Microwave	0	Hardwood	0	Other		0
Range	0	Vinyl	403	Other		0
Refrigerator	0	Subtotal	1,551	Painting: Exterior		700
Subtotal	0			Painting: Interior		1,000
		Foundation	0	Permits		0
Architectural Drawings	0	Framing	0	Subtotal		1,950
Cabinets	1,950	Garage	0			
Caulking	0	Gas & Electric Hookup	0	Plumbing		
Subtotal	1,950	Glass: Mirrors, showers	250	Commodes		0
		Gutters	200	Drain Lines		0
Cement Work		Subtotal	450	Faucets		250
Basement Floor	0			Fixtures		0
Driveway	0	HVAC		Hot Water Heater		0
Garage Floor	0	Air Conditioner	0	Showers		0
Porches	100	Duct Work	0	Tubs		0
Sidewalks	0	Filters	10	Water Lines		250
Subtotal	100	Furnace	250	Subtotal		500
		Subtotal	260			
Cleaning	250			Roofing		2,500
Counter Tops	270	Insulation	0	Siding		0
Decorating	0	Insurance Premiums	350	Site Planning & Engineering		0
Doors	250	Subtotal	350	Steel		0
Drywall	100			Trim		100
Electrical	100	Landscaping		Utility: Gas & Electric		375
Engineering	0	Irrigation System	0	Utility: Water & Sewer		125
Equipment Rental	350	Lot Clearing	250	Warranty		0
Excavation Work	0	Mowing Services	150	Windows		700
Fences	0	Sod	0	Subtotal		3,800
Fireplace	0	Trees, Plants, & Shrubs	150			
Subtotal	1,320	Subtotal	550	Total Cost of Improvements		12,781

Comp #1		Comp #2		Comp #3	
Address:		Address:		Address:	
Sales Price	58,900.00	Sales Price	54,000.00	Sales Price	70,000.00
Adjustments to Price	0.00	Adjustments to Price	26,400.00	Adjustments to Price	0.00
Adjusted Price	58,900.00	Adjusted Price	80,400.00	Adjusted Price	70,000.00
Square Feet	720.00	Square Footage	1,091.00	Square Feet	927.00
Price Per Square Foot	81.81	Price Per Square Foot	73.69	Price Per Square Foot	75.51

Comp Averages		Subject Property 2013 Wood Ln			Adjustment to Comps	5.00	
				Description	Best Case	Most Likely	Worst Case
Sales Price	60,966.67			Est Sales Price	71,425	67,040	62,655
Adjustments to Price	8,800.00	Square Feet	877.00	Purchase Price	22,950	22,950	22,950
Adjusted Price	69,766.67	Price/Sq Ft	26.17	Improvements	12,781	12,781	12,781
Square Feet	912.67	Imprvmnts/Sq Ft	14.57	Interest Charges	701	701	701
Price Per Square Foot	76.44	Total Price/Sq Ft	40.74	Taxes	450	450	450
				Closing Costs	3,643	3,643	3,643
Turn Comps Off/On	ON			Total Costs	40,525	40,525	40,525
Est Price/Sq Ft If Turned OFF	72.50	Estimated Time To		Profit Margin	30,901	26,516	22,131
WWW.THEVALUEPLAY.COM - COPYRIGHT PROTECTED 1998		Complete Project	4.00	Return On Inv	864.80%	742.08%	619.36%

yet another component to the purchase option by combining the basic lease or rental agreement with an option to purchase contract. Those investors who have the patience and skill to act as an intermediary between the homeowner and the lender can learn to master the art of the short sale and use this crucial technique to turn a deal with no apparent equity in it into a lucrative transaction. The subject to method of purchasing property benefits investors because the technique is quick and efficient, reduces transaction costs, enables the property to be easily transferred with a quitclaim deed, and permits the seller's credit to be salvaged when possible. Finally, loans made by private moneylenders represent an important source of financing that is usually not available through more traditional sources. Private moneylenders provide loans that are easier to obtain, offer investors greater flexibility, and provide up to 100 percent financing. The skilled investor employing the high-leverage techniques described in this chapter can achieve remarkable success with minimal risk and very little capital, thereby realizing maximum profits on a continuing basis.

PART 4

Epilogue

12

Put On the Armor of Success

In one of my previous books entitled *The Complete Guide to Buying and Selling Apartment Buildings,* I discussed what I referred to as the "five keys of success." These important keys of success addressed the need to:

- Properly understand risk
- Overcome your fear of failure
- Accept responsibility for your actions
- Have the willingness to persevere
- Define your sense of purpose

Although the book was intended to provide a comprehensive study and analysis of apartment buildings, I received more correspondence from individuals who were inspired by this discussion than correspondence on any other material in the book—a factor that I believe largely contributed to its success. I cannot help but feel that the hand of Providence guides my writing from time to time because thoughts flow freely from my heart and mind with little or no effort on my part. The concluding chapter of this book is no exception. In this chapter, I will discuss the necessity of putting on the armor of success. Although a suit of armor really has nothing to do with real estate, it has everything to do with your success. For that matter, putting on the armor of success can be applied to any business or profession and is not just limited to real estate. The precepts contained within this concluding chapter can be used in both your professional and personal life and, when properly applied, can be a source of great joy and happiness to you and to those with whom you associate.

The Armor of Success

For more than 5,000 years, armor has been used by both ancient and modern warriors to protect vital parts of their bodies in times of battle. Helmets worn by soldiers are depicted on Sumerian monuments dating back to 3000 BC. In the eleventh century BC, Chinese soldiers were known to have used armor made from several layers of rhinoceros skin to protect their bodies. Centuries later, mail armor, which is made of links of chain relatively impervious to the slashing strokes of a sword, was worn throughout the Roman Empire and lasted well into the fourteenth century AD. Other types of armor included brigandine suits used primarily for ceremonies, lamellar suits made of numerous narrow plates worn by the Persians, and various combinations of plate and mail armor worn by European, Turkish, and Russian knights, as well as many others. The four main components of a soldier's suit of armor were the helmet, breastplate, shield, and sword. Each one of these parts served a vital role in protecting the life of the soldier. While the helmet and breastplate were especially designed to protect the body, the shield and the sword were used to defend oneself against an enemy by protecting oneself with the shield while simultaneously dealing a series of strikes and blows with the sword to one's opponent. As modern day methods of warfare developed, the need for full suits of armor greatly diminished because they are incapable of protecting the body against advanced weaponry, such as shells fired from automatic weapons or rocket launchers. Although the use of complete suits of armor has dwindled over the years, the helmet is the primary piece of equipment that has stood the test of time. It is still worn today by men and women serving in various military units throughout the world.

While armor-plated suits remain relics of the past, there is much to be learned from them. Each piece of the suit was designed to protect a certain part of the body, with the exception of the sword, which was used to strike blows at one's opponents in an effort to defeat them. Suits of armor, necessary for the very survival of the ancient warriors who wore them, are just as necessary for the survival of modern day real estate investors. And just as each piece of armor served a unique and vital purpose for the warriors of old, so do they serve a unique and vital purpose for investors of today. First is the helmet, designed to protect the face and head, the source from which knowledge and intelligence stem. Next is the breastplate, intended to safeguard the chest and vital organs, the source from which courage and heroism stem. The shield, devised to be worn about the arm to frustrate blows from one's opponent, gives rise to the need for faith. Last is the sword, designed to strike down the enemy—the means by which justice is meted out. When used in harmony with one another, the helmet of knowledge, the breastplate of courage, the shield of faith, and the sword of justice arm the warrior with an invincible strength capable of defeating any opponent. Those individuals investing in real estate will also face many challenges, but like the knights of old, they must prepare for battle by arming themselves with the essential pieces of the suit of armor. The modern day real estate investor must fasten the helmet of knowledge securely about the head, he must wear the breastplate of courage about his chest, he must secure the shield of faith about his arm, and, finally, he must take up the sword of justice and be prepared to smite the enemy. The modern day real estate investor must *put on the armor of success.*

Helmet of Knowledge

The *helmet of knowledge* is the first essential element of the armor of success. The helmet has been worn by soldiers for thousands of years and is designed to protect the face and head, the source from which knowledge and intelligence flows. Blows to the unprotected head could literally strike opponents senseless, thereby rendering them incapable of defending themselves. Just as the helmet was crucial to the very survival of those individuals who wore them, so is the helmet of knowledge crucial to the very survival of those individuals desiring to be successful in the world of real estate investing. For that matter, success in any aspect of life, whether it be business, family, spiritual, physical, or personal, is directly dependent on obtaining useful knowledge that appropriately addresses the subject matter to which it applies. Knowledge, however, is incomplete and ineffective if the one who attains it fails to act upon it. It is instead the *application of knowledge* that allows one to soar to magnificent heights, to accomplish lifelong dreams, and to discover his true potential. Knowledge is like an instrument in the hands of wisdom. It must be picked up and used to be effective. While putting on the helmet of knowledge empowers us to achieve remarkable feats, it does not come without effort. It should be clearly understood that knowledge is not attained by random, unintended, or unpredictable events, but instead must be sought after with intense fervor and pursued with impassioned and relentless diligence. The pursuit of knowledge is not an isolated event that occurs once in our lives, but is instead a series of events that occurs throughout our entire lives. It is an ongoing and lifelong pursuit, even an eternal pursuit.

Once we have attained some degree of knowledge as it applies to a particular subject, it is the truth of that subject matter that transcends any external form of control that may be imposed upon us against our wills. In other words, the truth allows us to be free to act independently of what others may say or think about us. Knowledge and truth embolden us to act according to our own wills, not the wills of others.

The development of our ability to think independently and exercise judgment should be foremost in our efforts to attain knowledge. This is not to say that you should ignore the advice of others, but rather that you should listen carefully to what others have to say, and then be free to determine for yourself the proper course of action. Speaking about this particular topic, Albert Einstein once said, "Great spirits have always found violent opposition from mediocrities. The latter cannot understand it when a man does not thoughtlessly submit to hereditary prejudices but honestly and courageously uses his intelligence." Each of you has been blessed with your own unique set of gifts and talents. Each of you possesses tremendous potential just waiting to be unlocked. You must be willing, however, to insert the key of knowledge in order to open the door of opportunity. As you pursue your own dreams and goals in life, I encourage you to set aside time each and every day to enlighten your mind with the truth and light contained in the many good works written by men and women so that you, too, may *put on the helmet of knowledge.*

Breastplate of Courage

The *breastplate of courage* is the second essential element of the armor of success. The breastplate is intended to safeguard the chest and vital organs, the source of courage and heroism. Just as breastplates were crucial to the very survival of those individuals who wore them, so is the breastplate of courage crucial to the survival of those investors desiring to be successful in real estate. *Courage*, the angel of light, is the antithesis of that demon of darkness we call *fear*. The demon of darkness seeks our utter destruction as he whispers thoughts of discouragement into our ears. He tells us that we are weak, that we can't do it, and that we will surely fail. He tells us that others will think we don't know what we are doing, that we are wasting our time with such foolish pursuits, and that people will laugh at us. Fear is cunningly treacherous as he would like nothing more than to drag us down into the jaws of hell.

Fear strikes at the very heart, delivering unrelenting blows against the breastplate, hoping that he may eventually penetrate it and expose the organs. He knows that on doing so, they will become vulnerable and subject to complete and total decimation by him. Deep within each of us, however, lies an inner reservoir of strength known as courage, the angel of light. It is courage that gives us the ability to defeat fear.

Courage is not the absence of fear, but rather the mastery of it. When we purposely draw upon this inner reservoir of strength, fear has no choice but to be conquered. As courage and fear collide, the former will always prevail over the latter, provided we have donned that crucial piece of armor known as the breastplate of courage, for it is the breastplate that protects us from the otherwise fatal blows of fear. Courage is an imperial quality found only among those who wear its breastplate. It is the foundation upon which true achievement is based. Unless we have the moral fortitude to live out our convictions, courage is of little value. As you learn to draw upon your own inner reservoir of strength, remember that courage is not the absence of fear, but the mastery of it. As you seek to achieve noble and honorable goals throughout your life, do not leave yourself vulnerable to the demon of darkness. Rather, *put on the breastplate of courage* so that you can enjoy success in the pursuit of excellence as it applies not only to your real estate profession, but to all aspects of your life as well.

Shield of Faith

The *shield of faith* is the third essential element of the armor of success. The shield, devised to be worn about the arm to frustrate blows from one's opponent, gives rise to the need for faith. Just as the shield was crucial to the very survival of those individuals who wore them, the shield of faith is crucial to the very survival of those investors desiring to be successful in real estate. Faith is so important, in fact, it is necessary for our very survival. The shield of faith protects us from the fiery darts of the adversary who seeks our utter destruction. The adversary wants nothing more than to see us fail and to have us conclude, "I can't do it. I give up. I quit." James Freeman Clarke once said, "All the strength and force of man comes from his faith in things unseen. He who believes is strong; he who doubts is weak. Strong convictions precede great actions." So the principle of faith requires a belief in something or someone. Furthermore, that belief must be supported by strong feelings or a strong conviction to be effective. The principle of faith is not something that is developed overnight, but rather, it starts as a tiny seed and grows over time. When watered and nourished with thoughts and feelings of positive reinforcement, the seed begins to grow in such a way that it will help the individual in all aspects of his or her life. This means the mind must be fed a constant diet of uplifting thoughts and affirmations. If the mind is instead watered and nourished with thoughts and feelings of negative reinforcement, the seed will still grow but will hinder rather than help the individual.

My oldest son, Philip, learned to ride his bicycle when he was six years old, which is about average for most kids. Some learn when they are a little younger and some learn when they are a little older. When Philip finally made up his mind that he was going to learn to ride his bike, his tenacious attitude and dogged determination strengthened his faith and resolve in himself which, in turn, enabled him to claim victory over his opponent, the bicycle. The very moment Philip made up his mind that he was going to learn to ride his bike, his belief in himself, his faith, empowered him in such a way that he was able to complete the task that same day. One of my younger sons, Samuel, is now six years old. Samuel has not yet convinced himself that he can successfully ride a bicycle. He does not yet have the faith in his ability that he needs in order to learn to ride. As his father, I have tried to convince him otherwise, but with little success. I've told him repeatedly, "Sammy, I know you can do this. You're big enough to ride and will have no problem learning to balance yourself." My little Sammy, however, is not buying it. He refutes my assertions and claims just the opposite as he adamantly tells me, "Dad! I can't do it! I just can't do it!" And he's exactly right. He can't do it, and he won't be able to do it until he convinces himself, until he has the faith, that he can do it. Remember, the mind is a powerful tool as it does exactly what we tell it to. *We are who we think we are. We become who we think we can become. We are the product of our thoughts.* If you fail to put on the shield of faith and instead allow your mind to be dominated by destructive thoughts, these thought patterns will surely be transmuted into negative actions. Recall the adage, *"The thought precedes the action."* This statement is so powerful that even the forces of nature cannot deny its truth. Rather than allow your mind to be filled with negative thoughts, find ways to flood your mind with positive and uplifting thoughts that will be so pervasive and all-encompassing that they will have no choice but to awaken the genius that already exists within you. Feel the power and strength that surges through your body as your mind is inundated with affirmative and inspiring thoughts that will exalt you to a level of success in your life that you always knew existed, but were not sure of how to discover it. *Faith* is unquestionably the third essential element of the armor of success needed for each of us to achieve that which we are truly capable of, to awaken the genius that already exists within us. I say to each of you, *quench the fiery darts of the adversary* and, in so doing, you will soon begin to discover that the results of your positive thoughts will be greatly magnified, giving you cause to celebrate and rejoice in who you already are and in who you truly can become. Put on the *shield of faith* and enjoy all the rich and wonderful blessings life has to offer!

Sword of Justice

The *sword of justice* is the fourth essential element of the armor of success. The sword, designed to strike down the enemy when it becomes necessary, is the means by which justice is meted out. Just as the sword was crucial to the very survival of those individuals who wielded them in their defense, so is the sword of justice crucial to the very survival of those investors desiring to be successful in real estate. To better understand this principle, we must understand what is meant by the term *justice*. Justice is the state, action, or principle of treating all persons equally in accordance with the law. Justice implies that there exists a sense of fairness and equity in all things. Of course, we know this isn't true or, at least, it appears this is not the case. How many of us have gone through life and asked ourselves at one time or another the question, "Why me?" Or perhaps, "What have I done to deserve this?" Or maybe, "Why is this happening to me?" It would seem that the laws of justice are aligned directly against us and will do everything within their power to drag us down into a gulf of misery and hell. Instead of believing that life's forces are against us, allow me to be so bold as to suggest that we make a tectonic shift in our thinking by believing that life's forces are actually for us and not against us. Instead of asking ourselves the question, "Why me?" rephrase the question to ask, "Why *not* me?" Our lives would not be complete without adversity in them. Rather than asking ourselves, "What have I done to deserve this?" we can instead respond in a positive manner by recognizing that we have been blessed with yet another opportunity for growth. Justice is meted out according to our response to the many battles and challenges we will face in the short time we are here upon the earth. If we choose to whine and complain about how unfair life is, then we have learned nothing and are no better off for the opportunity given us. If, however, we choose to accept what appears to be an unjust event thrust upon us from on high as an opportunity to learn and grow from the experience, then I assure you that the outcome of the event will be markedly different from an alternatively negative response.

So there you have it. The fourth essential element of the armor of success is the sword of justice. The mighty sword is used to mete out justice against the seeming inequities that occur throughout our lives. Adversity is the great refiner's fire of life, which is used to temper and condition our souls. The refiner, much like a blacksmith, skillfully shapes and fashions the hot steel to strengthen and refine it, preparing it for the great battles of life. Whether or not our challenges arise from internal or external sources is irrelevant. What is really important is how we respond to them. When the storm rages and the rain descends upon us, when dark clouds have gathered their forces and the day is as black as night, when it seems that all is about to be lost and we will surely be swallowed up in the depths of the violent sea, as if by a miracle the heavens open in response to our pleadings to the great refiner of life. The sunlight bursts forth in brilliant shafts of light flooding our souls with warmth and renewing our sense of hope. The brightly colored rainbow, a magnificent prism in the sky, is the sign given by the refiner that all is well and that order has been restored. The impassioned storm, now past, has cleansed and purified the atmosphere, leaving behind an azure sky that is crisp, blue, and pristine. The beauty reflected by the earth, having transformed itself, now evokes feelings of joy and gladness within us. And so it is with each of us. As we chart our course through life, we will surely be tossed about by the violent tempests of life we know as adversity. If we just stay the course, our hearts and minds will be bathed in radiant beams of sunlight, reassuring us that all is well. If we will but wield the *sword of justice* when called upon to do so, we will surely be on the side of victory, and all things will come together for our good.

In summary, the suit of armor, which was necessary for the survival of the ancient soldiers who wore them, is just as necessary for the survival of real estate investors today. The suit of armor worn by real estate investors is referred to as the armor of success and comprises four essential elements. First is the helmet, which is designed to protect the face and head, the source from which knowledge and intelligence stem. Once obtained, it is the application of this knowledge that allows us to discover our true potential and to reach the goals we have set for ourselves. Second is the breastplate, which is intended to safeguard the chest and vital organs, the source from which courage and heroism stem. Courage is not the absence of fear, but rather the mastery of it. The third essential element of the armor of success is the shield, which is devised to be worn about the arm to frustrate the blows of an opponent, to protect us from the fiery darts of the adversary, giving rise to the need for faith. To achieve your real estate goals, fill your mind with positive and encouraging thoughts blended with impassioned emotions. Finally, the fourth essential element of the armor of success is the sword, which is designed to strike down the enemy when it becomes necessary and is the means by which justice is administered. Pick up the sword of justice, rise above the enemy, and conquer the foe. When used in harmony with one another, the helmet of knowledge, the breastplate of courage, the shield of faith, and the sword of justice will arm you with invincible strength capable of meeting any challenge. Finally, remember the principle introduced in Chapter 1, the *principle of balance*. Do not allow yourself to be so consumed with seeking wealth that the many other responsibilities you have, such as family, church, school, civic, and social duties, become out of balance. As a properly balanced real estate investor seeking opportunities in undervalued properties, you must put on the *armor of success* to truly be successful, to reach your full potential, and to achieve all that you are capable of.

Afterword

About Symphony Homes

Symphony Homes is one of Michigan's premier builders of high-quality new homes. We maintain a tradition of excellence by ensuring that each and every home we build meets our strict standards of quality. Symphony Homes is built on a foundation of three principals: quality, value, and service. From start to finish, we take care to ensure that only the best materials and the finest craftsmanship are utilized throughout the construction process. By partnering with key suppliers and efficiently managing our resources, we can effectively create value for home buyers by offering superior homes at competitive prices. Offering personal service to home buyers and fulfilling commitments to them allows us to provide each and every customer with an enjoyable building experience.

As a custom builder, Symphony Homes builds on home sites owned by individuals or those owned by the company. We offer new home construction services in all of Genesee County, Lapeer County, and North Oakland County.

For More Information

For information regarding Symphony Homes, one of Michigan's premier builders, please log on to www.symphony-homes.com.

Current ordering information for The Value Play Rental House Analyzer, Rehab Analyzer, Income Analyzer, Refi Analyzer, and other real estate products can be found at www.thevalueplay.com.

Index

Index

Index

Index

Index

Positive cash flow, 11
Positive reinforcement, 197–198
Postforeclosure market, 97–100
Preforeclosure opportunities, 89–92
Prerecorded message, 48
Presales, 111
Price appreciation, 7–8
Principal loan balance, 8–11
Principle of balance, 23–24
Principles of the enlightened millionaire, 21
Private money loan, 181–186
Professional associations, 43–46, 149
Property management firms, 16
Public records, 72, 97
Publications, 49–50, 149
Purchase options, 164–168
Purchasing information, 79–80

Q
Quitclaim deed, 178

R
Real estate agents:
    autopilot, 138–143
    classified ads, 51
    competency, 140–142
    fear of personal investment, 45
    postforeclosure properties, 99–100
    retailers, as, 148
    transferred employees, 70
    wholesalers, as, 145
Real estate appraisers, 44
Real estate developers, 102–105
Real estate investment:
    benefits, 6–12
    investment opportunities (*see* Finding investment opportunities)
    real estate market outlook, 15–20
    valuation, 25–37
        (*See also* Real estate valuation)

Real estate investment clubs, 51–52, 150
Real estate market outlook, 15–20
Real estate options (*see* Options)
Real estate owned (REO) portfolio, 35, 49, 97–98
Real estate products (Symphony Homes), 204
Real Estate Promo.com, 52
Real estate publications, 49–50, 149
Real estate valuation, 25–37
    appraisal, 26–27
    income capitalization method, 34–35, 121
    influencing factors, 28
    replacement cost method, 33
    sales comparison method, 35–36, 121
Real GDP growth, 15
Redemption period, 94–97
Redemption rights, 95–96
Refiner, 199–200
Regional trends, 16
    (*See also* States, U.S.)
Rehab Analyzer, 186
Relativity of value, 29–32
Relocation/transfer, 69–71
REO portfolio, 35, 49, 97–98
Replacement cost method, 33
Resell time, 16
Retailers, 146–148
Retirement, 77–80
Rightsizing, 73–75
Roman Empire, 192

S
Sales comparison method, 35–36, 121
Scouts, 143–144
Search engines, 50
Section 1031 tax-deferred exchange, 52–54
Seller distress (*see* Distressed sellers)

210

Index

Selling notes at discount, 173–174
Shareholder value, 20
Sheriff's sale, 92–94
Shield of faith, 196–198
Short sale, 172–176
Single family-to-commercial office conversion, 120–123
Single family-to-condominium conversion, 133–136
Single family-to-multifamily conversion, 123–124
Soldier's suit of armor, 192
Spacious foyers, 59
Spec houses, 110
Spillover effect, 13, 61
Spiritual beliefs, 20–23
Spread, 182
State taxes, 19
States, U.S.:
  new construction permits, 17
  population growth, 18, 19
  tax structure, 19
Subject to technique, 90, 177–181
Success, keys to, 191
  (*See also* Armor of success)
Suit of armor, 192
Super-adequacy, 58–59
Swimming pool, 30–31
Sword of justice, 198–200
Symphony Homes, 42, 122, 203

T
Tax exchange networks, 52–54, 150
Taxation:
  depreciation, 11
  IRC Section 1031 tax exchange, 52–54
  options, 161
  state taxes, 19

Texas, 18
Text, overview, 6
Title search, 178
Title theory state, 91, 95
Traffic, 61
Transfer/relocation, 69–71
Truth, 45, 194

U
Undervalued properties pipeline, 137
Uplifting thoughts, 197–198

V
Vacant houses, 56–57
Vacant on lock box (VLB), 70
Valuation, 25–37
  (*See also* Real estate valuation)
Value, 5, 28–32, 140
Value Play Rehab Analyzer, 186
Visibility adds value, 63–64
VLB (vacant on lock box), 70

W
Wal-Mart, 19–20
Waterfalls and streams, 58–59
Weather, 16, 18, 114
Web sites:
  InfoUSA, 75
  marketing campaign, 150
  real estate investment clubs, 52
  Symphony Homes, 204
  (*See also* Internet)
Wholesalers, 145–146
Wood Lane property analysis, 187
Work-home balance, 23–24

Y
Yahoo!, 50

About the Author

Steve Berges is a real estate investment professional with over 25 years of experience. As principal of Symphony Homes, he is an active investor specializing in creating value through various real estate mechanisms, including single-family houses, multifamily apartment complexes, and the development and construction of single-family and condominium housing communities. Berges holds an MBA degree in finance and marketing from Rice University. He is also the author of *The Complete Guide to Investing in Rental Properties*, as well as many other popular books on real estate.